2.00

D0893727

Memories are made of this

Memories are made of this

Melinda McCracken

James Lorimer & Company, Publishers
Toronto 1975

ISBN: 0-88862-076-4

Cover design: Lynn Campbell

James Lorimer & Company, Publishers
35 Britain Street
Toronto

Printed and bound in Canada

Canadian Shared Cataloguing in Publication Data

McCracken, Melinda
    Memories are made of this / Melinda McCracken. —

1. McCracken, Melinda.   2. Winnipeg —
Social life and customs.   I. Title.

CT310.M24A3   928.2
ISBN: 0-88862-076-4

Contents

Dedication

To the 1957 graduating class of Churchill High School.

Acknowledgements

I would like to thank Karen Wood, Brenda Reimer, Maureen Pederson, John Kemp, Lionel Moore, Irene and Murray Brueckner, John and Marianne Hodges, Mr. W. J. Madder, Bill Porter, Terry Gray, The Ontario Arts Council and all who helped in making this book possible.

M.M.

I Introduction

Out Osborne Street

Winnipeg is one of the flattest cities anywhere. Like most cities, it has its north, east, south and west parts, to which people informally refer and by which they orient themselves. Each part has acquired an identity of its own, and each implies a certain economic level. Because of the flatness, directions are indicated by 'out' rather than 'up at' or 'over in'.

The north end, 'out Main Street', and across the Salter Street Bridge, is immigrant and ethnic, with its Jews, Germans, Poles, Ukrainians, Icelandics, Swedes, Metis and Indians living side by side. Most of the City's new growth has taken place in the west end, 'out Portage Avenue'; towards the City of St. James Portage Avenue becomes a strip of pancake houses, car lots, drive-in restaurants, and gas stations; high rises and middle-class suburbs such as Silver Heights have grown up there too. North of Portage, the west end is older and working-class. There is no east end as such, as the east end was always St. Boniface, a separate city of French Canadians. But since St. Boniface's amalgamation with Metro Winnipeg in 1971, English-speaking Winnipeggers have moved into its suburbs, Windsor Park and Southdale. The south end includes Winnipeg's most affluent areas, River Heights, Tuxedo and the less affluent Fort Rouge; the south end is generally associated with the middle and upper-middle classes. The outlying suburbs of Winnipeg are referred to by their official names—Elmwood, Norwood, East, North and South and West Kildonan, Fort Garry, Wildwood Park, Charleswood, Transcona and Selkirk.

Fort Rouge is south of the Assiniboine River, west of the Red River and east of Pembina Highway. It is named after a fort which used to stand at the forks of the Red and Assiniboine rivers and which was built in 1738 by a merchant named Delamarque. The fort was actually called The Forks by La Verendrye and Delamarque, but a 1740 mapmaker decided on Fort Rouge. The area was an independent community called West St. Boniface until 1882, when it was incorporated into the City of Winnipeg, and named, by the city council, Fort Rouge.

Fort Rouge is the south end, out Osborne Street. (In Winnipeg, avenues run east and west, and streets run north and south.) Osborne runs from Portage Avenue southeast until it hits the Red River. The Red runs east across the foot of the street, then loops back west in a big horseshoe and continues to flow north to Lake Winnipeg. The horseshoe encloses the school district of Riverview. West of Osborne is a triangular area contained by railroad tracks, the Pembina Highway and the Red River; this is the Lord Roberts school district. Riverview and Lord Roberts school districts together comprise South Fort Rouge.

In the late 1880s and early 1900s the two focal points of South Fort Rouge were the Fort Rouge Yards and an amusement park called River Park, located on the banks of the Red at the foot of Osborne Street. The yards, built in the first decade of the twentieth century as the main shops of the Canadian Northern Railway (later part of the CNR), filled the tip of the right-angle triangle west of Osborne Street, where their huge 212-foot smokestack was a familiar landmark.

River Park opened as a race track in 1893 and offered racing winter and summer. It was owned by James Bert Austin, who also operated horsedrawn streetcars after 1882 and electric cars after 1891. The first extension of the electric line, called the Park Line, was made along Osborne Street to River Park, and it was used to transport merrymakers and picnickers to the park. In 1894 the Winnipeg Electric Street Railway Company bought out Austin's interest in both the street railway and River Park. The amusement site soon began to celebrate the glories of the age of Edison with new delights—whippets racing after an electric hare, electric horses that revolved around a track, six in a row, and electric lights—and for more than forty years was one of Winnipeg's favourite entertainment areas. It had western Canada's first zoo, a roller coaster, a carousel, flying boats, and rope-pulled swings for boys to swing their sweethearts on. A miniature train on a tiny track pulled people around the park. People drank sarsaparilla, but off Jubilee Avenue was a bootlegger who sold beer under the counter of an ice cream parlour. There was a baseball park, and in winter a track was cleared on the ice for harness racing with sulkies. There was a skating rink and a toboggan slide, dog-team races and snow-shoeing on the Red River.

The Red River is flat and wide, its brown face dimpled with

eddies and currents. It flows by green Manitoba ashleaf maples and elms on banks of Red River gumbo, a grey muddy clay that dries and cracks on top but stays gooey underneath. Along the banks, by River Park, trails and cracked mud paths snaked through the bushes; here lovers cycled or strolled in the light of the silvery moon. Leading across the river to St. Vital was a romantic pontoon footbridge, a seasonal wooden span with chicken-wire sides, strung with electric lights. Lovers could pay a five-cent toll charge and walk over to the other side. Further west was another trestle tollbridge, the Elm Park Bridge, built by Americans in 1912 as an investment.

Contained within natural boundaries cutting it off from the rest of the city, South Fort Rouge has always been very stable. The railroaders settled on the west side of Osborne Street, to be near their work at the yards. On streets near the yards, houses are grouped close together on twenty-five-foot lots; they are quaint wooden bungalows with glassed-in verandahs, and each is definitely separate from, though close to, the next. From the south side of Rathgar Avenue, south to Jubilee, the houses are large, three storeys high and wooden; some have barn-shaped roofs, and glassed-in verandahs; they rest on fifty-foot lots and are very close together but detached. The trees were planted in 1919, about the time most of the houses were built. Jubilee was named after Queen Victoria's 1897 Diamond Jubilee, which celebrated her sixty years on the English throne.

Many of the other landmarks on the west side were built around the turn of the century. The barns where streetcars were serviced were built just south of Morley Avenue in 1906. Lord Roberts School, an imposing grey stone structure named after Earl Frederick Sleigh Roberts, a British field marshal famous for his achievements in Afghanistan in the late nineteenth century, was built in 1910. Rosedale United Church, originally Rosedale Methodist Church, was built in 1910 by money raised by district Methodists. St. Alban's Anglican Church at Osborne and Rathgar was built in 1910. In about 1913 the firehall at the corner of Arnold and Osborne was built. The firemen lived in and the hose wagon and ladder truck were pulled by horses. Bernard C. Juby opened the Fort Rouge Pharmacy at Rosedale and Osborne in 1913, and the Fort Rouge Curling Club was built in 1919 at Kylemore and Osborne.

The east side of Osborne Street, in the horseshoe formed by the Red River and known as Riverview, is quite different. Except for houses on Morley Avenue, which rest on twenty-five-foot lots, Riverview houses have fifty-foot lots; they are set quite far apart, and built of brick or stucco, with River Park occupying the area south of Clare Avenue to the river bank. The Clare Avenue home of the River Park police officer, Mr. Ottensen, and several other three-storey homes with turrets and large verandahs were built, to be followed by smaller stucco houses on the lots between. Riverview School, in the middle of the area, was constructed in 1908, and was the first school erected in South Fort Rouge. The original frame Riverview United Church was built in 1907 on two lots purchased for a dollar near the corner of Oakwood Avenue and Osborne Street. In the east part of the horseshoe formed by the curve of the Red River, a temporary hospital, called 'The San', was opened for advanced tuberculosis cases in 1911. In 1912 H.R.H. The Duke of Connaught, Canada's Governor General, and his daughter, Princess Patricia, opened the King Edward Memorial Hospital nearby, and at the same time officiated at the laying of the cornerstone of the King George Hospital, which opened in 1914.

And so, duly endorsed by the British Empire, the foundations of South Fort Rouge, both the working-class west side of Osborne and the middle-class east side, were laid. The district continued to grow as other buildings and other businesses were established. The Overlook Apartments, a newlywed set-up having romantic associations with River Park, were situated at the foot of Jubilee, so that their corniced facade peered between the trees, in much the same way as the Arc de Triomphe peers between the plane trees on the Champs Elysees. In 1925 Riverview Church replaced the original structure with a large red brick building boasting a small steeple and a rose window in the front facade. In a store between Baltimore Road and Ashland, a Polish couple, Peter and Anna Kozub, operated a snack bar called the Park Inn, on trade from River Park.

The Park Theatre, also named after River Park, began as the neighbourhood silent movie theatre. It was purchased in 1930 by Rudolph Besler, who installed sound equipment for talkies. The Beslers lived around the corner on Baltimore Road, and ran their theatre themselves. Mrs. Besler sold the tickets and Mr. Besler tore them in half. Admissions were ten cents for children, twenty-five for adults and five for the Saturday matinee. With the price of admission came a large round caramel sucker that usually lasted from the start of the movie until suppertime. During the Depression, when the United Church manse on Baltimore Road opened its doors to young men riding the rails in search of work,

Mr. Besler renovated his theatre, more to provide employment than to improve the premises. A Safeway food store opened next to the Park Theatre. The Winnipeg Public Library had a branch in the Beresford Apartments opposite, next to the Aldridge and Lamb Meat Market. The Riverview Hardware, on the other side of the movie house, was owned and operated by Charlie Wright, who lived on Ashland Avenue. Mr. Juby moved his drugstore to the main floor of the Beresford Apartments at Osborne and Beresford.

Lord Roberts Community Centre was founded in 1934 at the corner of Kylemore Avenue and Daly Street. Originally known as The Terriers, the club consisted of two boxcars donated by the CNR. Likewise, the Riverview Community Club, at Ashland and Eccles, got its start from the CNR which donated a boxcar as a place to change skates.

In 1941, the Winnipeg Electric Company sold the forty acres of land occupied by River Park, to a builder-developer, C.E. Simonite, who wanted to put up 250 homes on residential lots along the river bank, with two parallel east and west streets further back. He also planned to build 250 more homes on the twenty-odd acres east of Osborne, occupied by Elm Park.

So River Park closed. Its roller coaster and carousel were sold and moved. Ferris wheel seats and the little engine from the miniature train were stored in a wooden shack on the vacant land and in a shed by Mr. Ottensen's house. The area it occupied became overgrown with yellow grass, milkweed, alfalfa, Scotch thistles and goldenrod. Meadowlarks sang in the elm trees, sections of track where the little train had run still snaked through the yellow grass and pieces of sidewalk leading nowhere still remained. The foundations of the bear pits were still there.

The homes built by Simonite began to take form south of Jubilee on the west side. The houses were white stucco bungalows in the new American ranchstyle or the Cape Cod design. The contractor was careful to avoid sameness; he altered small details on each house, here varying the colour of the trim, the entrances, the roofs, there adding shutters to one picture window and leaving them off another. The houses were of three basic designs: a peaked-roof bungalow of one and a half storeys with an acute peak over the front door and a picture window on one side; a one-storey bungalow with a low roof and a picture window; and a two-storey box with two windows downstairs and two upstairs. All three designs had slab doors with one of several window patterns cut into them, the most common being three descending upright rectangles. The houses on the street facing the river were larger, had deeper lots and looked out on a boulevard of elms (the remains of Elm Park) and the river. The streets were named after Second World War generals: on the west side, after McNaughton and Montague, and, on the east, where River Park had been, after Montgomery and Wavell. The street circling the river, Churchill Drive, celebrated Winston.

People who'd grown up in small prairie towns moved into Winnipeg, often for economic reasons, in the twenties and thirties. These newcomers settled in South Fort Rouge. The working-class railroaders in their overalls and straw hats lived in the older houses on the west side. The middle class—former country school teachers, now married, civil servants, employees of Eaton's and of the head office of Great West Life, even the occasional doctor, barrister or a rare professor, as well as shop owners on Osborne Street—lived in Riverview. They had postponed making major moves until after the war. When the war was over, people threw away their sugar- and butter-rationing books and their war-saving stamps and dug in to have their children and make good lives for themselves; they talked about how good things had been 'before the war', but the new drive for home, security and family was on.

The C.E. Simonite houses on the east side of Osborne began to go up, and in the morning syncopated hammers banged as workmen put up roofs and shingles. The people who lived in the central part of Riverview were older than those who began to move into the new houses, but both groups started families after the war. Except for a small strip of land south of Churchill Drive, which ran from the foot of Osborne all the way around the area formerly occupied by River Park, Riverview was slowly eaten up by foundations. As people bought up the white stucco houses, the district continued to grow.

My parents moved into Riverview in 1944. Both my mother and father are former teachers who taught in small prairie towns before coming to Winnipeg. My father switched from teaching school to selling life insurance for Great West Life. I was four when they bought their house on Balfour Avenue. Two years later my brother John arrived. Nearby lived the Struthers, good friends of my parents. Ruth Struthers had grown up in Neepawa, gone to school with my mom and later taught school. Mr. Struthers was a barrister. They moved first to Rosedale, then to a house on Clare Avenue and finally to a stucco house on the corner of Ashland and Hay. They had one daughter, Frances, and a second daughter,

Susan, six years younger. Next door to the Struthers on Ashland lived Mr. and Mrs. Herman Carson. Both Mr. and Mrs. Carson had gone to art school at the University of Manitoba, and Mr. Carson worked in the display department at Eaton's and designed the annual Eaton's Santa Claus Parade. They had one daughter, Frances, a year older than Sue and I, and a son, Bob, two years younger. On the other side of Hay Street, on Ashland, the third house down, lived Mr. and Mrs. Wilson Kaye; Mr. Kaye worked for Winnipeg Supply and Fuel, a coal company. The Kayes had one son, Alan, and two daughters, Barbara, the same age as Sue Struthers and I, and Carolyn, several years younger.

All four families were middle class, had had baby girls in 1939 and 1940 and lived near each other. The four girls, Sue, Barb Fran and I, were friends from the very beginning.

II   *After the War*

Parents

Physically, Riverview was a stable place for parents to settle down and raise a family. The turf itself was dead flat, cut off from the city by Osborne Street and the surrounding river. There were stubby black-barked scrub oak trees, box elders (ashleaf or Manitoba maples), elm trees, lilac and honeysuckle bushes and plenty of sparrows, robins and brown squirrels to populate them. The yards were large, open and mostly unfenced and unhedged, and solidly in the middle of them sat the houses, at ample distances from one another. There were few cars and few people on the streets, and the ratio of open space to people and the sun- and shade-dappled grass gave the area an aura of privacy and dignity, although the houses themselves were not imposing.

But it was the people who lived in the houses that gave the area its sense of permanence and stability, solid respectable middle-class couples with growing children. Houses were landmarks. Taking home as centre, you mentally located families in a firm, specific place, behind, in front or on either side of you. People didn't move around; they were there, some of them, for life, and houses took on the qualities of the people living in them, some cozy and pretty, some rambling and untidy. Because of the long winters which isolated even the closest neighbours from one another, life in the houses was very private, with socializing between neighbours carried on only on a formal level or restricted to a few words over the back fence.

Most of the parents in the central part of Riverview were in their forties. Life in the small towns where they'd grown up had been influenced by the Methodist Church—and after 1924, when the Methodist, Presbyterian and Congregational Churches amalgamated, the United Church—Victorian morality, railroading and wheat farming. They had come from those prairie towns where rain and crops meant make or break, where the identity of the town was the grain elevator on the yellow horizon, and the empty boxcars waiting beside it; they could tell at a glance which crop was flax, barley, rye, oats or wheat, whether a farmer was seeding, threshing, baling or stooking and how the crops were doing.

In such towns the Methodist Church, based on the teachings of John Wesley who believed that the grace of God could transform every life that received it, preached the doctrine of conscious acceptance of God, of daily growth in holiness and victory over sin. Its appeal to the conscience was fairly strict: no gambling, no drinking, no card-playing and no work on Sunday. People cooked their roasts of beef on Saturday, and would serve only cold meat and do no work in the kitchen on Sunday. The singing of lay songs on Sunday was frowned upon, except for innocent favourites like 'Come Into the Garden Maude'. On Sunday people often went to church four times, a service in the morning, then Sunday School in the afternoon, then bible class and, after dinner at home, the evening service. Finally they went back to a fellow church member's house and sang hymns around the piano. People really believed wholeheartedly in God and took the teachings to heart. God was life, and the church gave people the laws of life.

The two secure refuges in life were the home and the church. Home was where the heart was. Families were large and children were considered a blessing. The church exhorted people to love their neighbours as themselves and to do good works, and people lived up to these decrees as best they could.

The natural biological pattern of life was sanctioned by the church's teachings. Young boy meets young girl, they fall in love, become engaged, are married, lose their virginity together and eagerly await the first child. The security of the children was ensured, and thus the healthy survival of the human race. The natural pattern acquired certain rituals—the engagement ring, the hope chest, the trousseau, the shower, the groom's stag and selecting the patterns of silverware, dinnerware, glassware and linen, chosen to last, for the permanent home the couple was making together. Then the church wedding, with her father giving the virgin bride over to the groom, who placed the wedding ring, symbol of the lifetime bond, on her finger; the honeymoon, the first 'suite', the purchase of the first home, the first child, the christening. The phrase 'doing well' was used to describe a young couple who were showing signs of becoming economically successful, money being a hard fact of life. Their standard of living was raised by the young man's efforts out in the world and the young woman's sewing, baking, mothering and housekeeping abilities at home. Marriage was a sacrament, a lifetime oath taken under the eyes of God, and, because it was sanctioned by Him, people trusted it; it was the only course. According to God, everything was supposed to work perfectly, furnishing health, security, wealth and happiness to husband-provider and housewife mother, on into middle age, retirement and old age, till death them did part.

The parents brought these beliefs and traditions with them into the city. In real terms, since marriage was the most efficient way of achieving the security necessary to raise children, and since security, not mobility, was what people needed and were drawn to, marriage gave most people what they wanted. It had more advantages than disadvantages, and on most levels it worked. How seriously people took the institution of marriage manifested itself in the way life was lived in Riverview.

There, people functioned socially as couples. They were known as the . . . s (the Struthers, the Carsons, the Wrights, the Kayes, the McCrackens). The husband, working at his job or profession, was away all day at the office making money. The wife raised the children and maintained the home. That was what was expected of people; marriage was more important than individual fulfilment, and in fulfilling the central role people's lives were justified.

What mattered was not the emotional quality of the marriage, or the happiness of its partners, but the fact of the marriage and its endurance. Since marriage was holy, it had to be right, and to admit it made one unhappy was a small voice against the authority of the church. Any chafing away at each other, any internecine sabotage, emotional blackmail or destructive game-playing between partners was never openly acknowledged. Nothing that was going on between people was talked about; it never really reached the point of verbalization, let alone escaped through the front door. People talked about traditional events and changes in others' lives—sickness, births, deaths, successes—but not their feelings. The marriage fact was the thing; the relationship was marriage.

So people did not leave their partners if they were unhappy. They accepted each other without complaint and played their roles well to the outside world. They toed the line all the way down, and whatever internal desperation they might suffer they never put into words. People who chose their marriage partners for life seldom got even an inkling of what their lives might have been like if they'd made a different choice. They'd made the choice and they simply could not know. People in this situation developed a lot of self-control and stoicism. Yet, protected and limited by their marriage, they thus remained rather innocent.

No one questioned the validity of monogamy. People simply made it work. Although affection, friendliness, neighbourliness, helpfulness, kindness, generosity and love poured out, the sexual relationship remained submerged within the marriage. Anything that threatened marriage, from flirting to adultery, was sinful. Drinking was sinful, and no one drank. Gambling was sinful, and no one gambled. Divorce was almost unknown, and when it occurred was too highly charged to be talked about. Whatever deviated from the norm was either sinful or exotic. The norm was very narrow.

Couples worked hard. Besides their roles as breadwinner and homemaker, the man and woman both worked hard on the home, building picket fences, clipping hedges, mowing the lawn, raking leaves, putting in plants, turning on sprinklers. The men wore toe rubbers, some of them even wore spats, and their socks were held up by garters, which vanished when socks learned to stay up by themselves. Their suits were squarely cut and voluminous, with long lapels, and wide trousers. They wore black overcoats and homburg hats. Their glasses were octagonal, with no rims. The wives wore nylons with seams in them, high heels, girdles, long-line bras, slips and dresses. They got their hair done weekly at Alma's or Sophie's Hair Styling. They baked cookies and cakes and dainties for school teas, and went to Home and School Association meetings. They wore seal, mouton or muskrat coats, overstockings, high-heeled overshoes, trimmed with fur, that laced up over their shoes, and like Queen Elizabeth they wore hats and gloves to church on Sunday and to school teas. Their fashions were demure, plain dresses, or suits with skirts and blouses, enhanced with a brooch at the neck to match their earrings. For this was a long, permanent life they were living; standards had to be high; things had to be done with deliberation, and the key word was responsibility. They golfed together in the summer, curled together in the winter and played bridge all year round.

Bridge also had roots that went back a long time to small-town life. They had played together as newlyweds, as young married couples and as parents. Neighbours in Riverview would get together on Saturday nights at one couple's house for a rubber of bridge. Since it is played in couples, bridge is a game that was ideally suited to the forms of marriage. It is a good game, and it has the enticement of being cards without being gambling. A bridge party usually consisted of two or four couples, who sat around tables with legs that folded up, and had covers that fitted and were held to the table by strips of elastic that stretched under its corners. The men wore their suits, and the women got dressed up. Manners were impeccable. The custom of changing tables and partners between hands enabled gentlemen to meet ladies, one partner to get an impression of what the other was like without the slightest violation of marital etiquette.

In fact, people who have been playing bridge over a long period of time have evolved it into a whirl of elegant manners and subtle signs. The way a lady crosses her legs and folds her skirt when she sits down does not go unnoticed by the gentleman across the table; the way she holds her cards, how well she plays them, the way she discusses them, the integrity with which she supports his hand, all these are clues to the kind of person she is. The rounds of changing tables, the patter that goes along with the game, the manners surrounding the coffee and sandwiches afterwards have all been refined to a very high level. Though bridge is only entertainment, it is around the game that practised players communicate.

My parents started out traditionally, as did the Struthers and many other couples in the neighbourhood. Their houses had traditional furniture and decor—a dark wood dining room suite, a buffet, a lace tablecoth, a china cabinet with glass doors behind which the china and silver were displayed, a tea wagon, a piano and so on. The Struthers on Ashland were traditional and British in lifestyle. Mr. Struthers was in the trenches in the First World War, and had photographs in frames in his den of his platoon in uniform. A short man with the trim square moustache of the times, glasses, plaid shirts and tweedy pants, he smoked a pipe and communicated a thoughtful tobaccoey presence. Mrs. Struthers, a particularly intelligent woman, wore her grey hair short and fingerwaved at the sides, and had an air about her that was simultaneously stern and humorous. In a sharkskin slack suit with a kerchief around her hair, she led us kids on wiener roasts and cheered us on off into the bushes to pick saskatoons and raspberries at Victoria Beach on Lake Winnipeg. The Struthers home featured dark traditional furniture and a big old grandfather clock. The Kaye home, a new yellow bungalow with dark red Tudor beams over the door, was smaller, and also furnished in the traditional manner. Mr. Kaye was a handsome dark-haired man and Mrs. Kaye was short with short hair.

The Carsons were different. Their lifestyle was American. They drank, copiously. Mr. Carson swore, boisterously. They'd travelled to unheard of places like New York, Florida and the Gulf of Mexico. They had a goldfish pond. The Carson house was stucco like many others, but the windows had been changed, and it was painted a mustardy yellow with soft blue trim. They had a sunporch and a sunroom. Mr. Carson remodelled the house himself with new materials like striated wood, and everything was built in, and done in lovely colours, yellows and soft blues. Even the wallpaper was special. The Carsons had rubber plants in their sunroom before rubber plants had even come to North America, it seemed. They had a bar in the basement. There were trees like a weeping birch, blue spruce and a Russian olive in the front yard that matched the house—that matched the house! The Carsons seemed always to be the first to have anything that was any good. And Mr. Carson had a lovely touch with colour and materials. We revered him as the Walt Disney of Riverview. In comparison with the traditional lifestyles around them, the Carsons were exotic, talented, mysterious, and seemed to have an awful lot of fun.

Authority

In the world we lived in, things were generally seen as being hierarchical. God was the supreme authority. People respected God and trusted in Him. This trusting respect for authority was transferred to authority at all levels. Authority per se was good. It helped one live the good life. You obeyed the rules, and goodness followed naturally. There were authority figures at many levels—fathers, teachers, principals, doctors, administrators, premiers and prime ministers, police chiefs, heads of companies. People believed in what they said and thought their intentions honourable.

Authority was based on position, not on the inherent superior knowledge, ability or achievement of the individual holding the position. It was assumed that a person with power had achieved something. It was desirable to attain authority, to go up ladders, and so wielding power over others was also desirable. As things stood in the hierarchy, many groups were considered to be lower in respectability than middle-class families of British stock or native Canadian ancestry. The poor, Jews, DP's, Uker-ainians and Roman Catholics were discriminated against. These prejudices were in many ways the mark of respectability. Blame was big. People in authority blamed the powerless, and the powerless were expected to respond by feeling guilty.

The attitudes of the times were parental. Parents were strong, responsible, mature people. The people they had power over were their children. However generous in other ways, parents assumed they knew best, that they had the right to control their children's lives and tell them what to do. Kids obeyed. Seen from a child's point of view, fathers were often terrifying, exercising the prerogatives of Victorian patriarchs, a role they'd assumed from their own fathers. Fathers were pushed around by their own superiors, upon whom they depended for a living and to whom they looked up. When they came home, they pushed their wives and kids around. Since a woman had vowed to love, honour and obey, she obeyed. At the same time, she was often perceived by the children to be oppressed by her husband, and she herself was sympathetic with the children and charitable to the downtrodden and the needy.

Part of the exercise of authority was to control the behaviour of others, and the fact that an authority figure was able to prevent those beneath him from doing something proved his power. When a father told his kid to do something, he assumed immediate compliance. If he was asked why, he answered, 'Because I said so.' This was reason enough, but was resented all the same by the kid who obeyed or was punished.

Church

The good people of Riverview went to church every Sunday in the neighbourhood, as they had done when they were growing up. The church was the real, spiritual centre of life, corresponding to the religious and spiritual impulse inside people. If you had religious or spiritual feeling of a force greater than man, or towards charity and love, the place to take it was to church. Church traditions were so familiar in the lives of people they were more or less taken for granted. Responsibility for the church's operation was taken by the community, and, except for the minister, the organist and the choir leader (and perhaps the tenor or soprano soloist), who were paid, the other participants in the church—choir members, Sunday school teachers, ushers, elders, stewards and trustees—worked voluntarily, feeling an obligation to serve God.

The service began at 11 a.m. on Sunday with the organist playing a processional as people took their seats in the pews. Men hung their overcoats in the cloakroom in the foyer, but the gloved and hatted women sat through the service with their black seal, mouton, muskrat or Persian lamb coats around their shoulders. This is a Winnipeg custom: you get so used to wearing your winter coat that you don't feel right when you take it off.

In the United Church, which had puritan country roots, ritual was suspect, and was associated with the Catholic Church. United Church rituals were anti-ritual, and United Church people were proud of this.

The service began with rising and singing 'Holy Holy Holy, Lord God Almighty'. The congregation sat down, and the minister asked them to turn to page so and so and sing hymn number 569; the numbers of the hymns to be sung were posted in black and white movable numbers on signs on each side of the altar. The people rose again, dark blue hymn books in hand, reading the words and following the organ for the tune; many of the people knew the tune by heart. The service would unfold, with the minister saying 'Let us pray', at which one and all rose with their heads bowed, as he said the prayer; they ended with the recitation of the Lord's Prayer. There was an anthem sung by the choir, then another hymn, after which the minister gave the news, or the 'Life and Work' of the church, as it was called in the mimeographed programme with the coloured picture of a Bible story on the outside.

Halfway through the service, men volunteers from the congregation took up the collection, passing a wooden collection plate, usually with a circle of green felt on it so as to muffle any jingling of coins. The collection plate was passed along one pew, and the volunteer would take it and pass it back to the next, until the four men would arrive back at the altar the moment the organist had finished his muted accompanying piece. People used envelopes perforated down the middle into two sections, one for their church and the other for external missions. The minister blessed the collection, and the money was removed to be dealt with later by the finance committee.

The service resumed with another hymn, or a response reading. The men in the congregation shyly read from their hymn books, and sang in harmonic bass notes in their particular range. The sound of the congregation singing, praying and reading in response to the minister was inimitable, the male and female voices starting off at different times, picking up, mumbling in monotone and falling away jaggedly; it was as if everyone in the congregation knew the precise blend of tedium and reverence that was necessary for the service to sound right. No one spoke, except in whispers. You stood and sang, knelt and prayed, sat down.

The minister's sermon was based on a verse in the Bible. The Sermon related the verse to a current event of some kind, and then drew a general conclusion about some aspect of life. Its theme often stressed what sinners we all were. The homily over, the service might then move into a choir anthem or a song by the soloist. Then the minister stood with his surpliced arms spread like wings, giving the benediction, for which all would rise and bow their heads. The organist played a bright postlude and people, talking softly, filed outside.

God was God the Father, God the Son, God the Holy Ghost. God the Father was the powerful patriarch whom people feared and obeyed. He was stern and sometimes unmerciful, like Old Man Winter, the archetypal authority figure before whom people became humble and bowed their heads. The Son, Christ, was the God of love, kinder and more tolerant, and God the Holy Ghost was not very well understood. It was God the Father whom one feared and obeyed, for disobeying His word was sinning and deserved punishment.

People going to church and worshipping God were absolutely sincere in what they were doing. People believed in the Ten Commandments, which were clearly excellent rules to follow in life; it was obvious how true they were and how simply they distinguished good from evil. People believed in the Beatitudes, in the Bible, and their belief was helpful to them. Of course, their belief had also to extend to the Immaculate Conception, Christ's crucifixion to save mankind, His rising on the third day from the dead, the parting of the Red Sea, the Burning Bush and the life everlasting. How exactly people imagined that everlasting life or related those miracles to their own lives was left to the imagination. But you didn't need explanation or understanding. You had only to believe and the church and the Bible gave expression to your belief.

The minister and the power of God, symbolized by the altar, the throbbing organ and the impressive pipes behind it, bore down on the congregation, exhorting people not to sin and warning them of the punishments. Naturally, most people in the congregation sinned regularly in small ways. In church they were made to feel guilty under the eyes of God, and received their punishment through the sermon.

Most of the kids in South Fort Rouge went to church with their parents, or at least to Sunday School, at Riverview or Rosedale United churches or St. Alban's Anglican. Usually, after the collection and before the sermon, the kids were let out to attend their Sunday school in the back. Or they returned in the afternoon. They received Sunday School papers with a picture of the story on the front and the story inside, and a Golden Text to learn. The papers had holes punched in the side, so you could tie them together and have all the stories of the Bible. We gathered in a circle on wooden chairs in our Sunday best, and learned from a young girl or one of the ladies about the black and yellow and red children around the world. We learned the Psalms and the Beatitudes and the Ten Commandments and read Hurlbut's Bible. We learned the parables and stories in the Old Testament and the tales of Jesus and sang children's hymns. The gentler side of the church was evident in the loving inspiration of the songs we sang:

> Tell me the stories of Jesus
> I love to hear;

Things I would ask Him to tell me
If He were here;
Scenes by the wayside,
Tales by the sea,
Stories of Jesus
Tell them to me.

—William Parker
© National Sunday School Union

Jesus wants me for a sunbeam,
To shine for Him each day;
In ev'ry way try to please Him
At home, at school, at play.
A sunbeam, a sunbeam,
Jesus wants me for a sunbeam;
A sunbeam, a sunbeam,
I'll be a sunbeam for Him.

—E. O. Excell. (Re-arranged by C. L. Naylor)

Hear the pennies dropping,
Listen while they fall;
Ev'ry one for Jesus,
He shall have them all.
Dropping, dropping, dropping, dropping,
Hear the pennies fall;
Ev'ry one for Jesus
He shall have them all.

—W. J. Kirkpatrick

Jesus bids us shine with a pure, clear light,
Like a little candle burning in the night;
In this world of darkness so we must shine;
You in your small corner, and I in mine

—Words by Susan Warner,
E. O. Excell.

Jesus loves me, this I know,
For the Bible tells me so;
Little ones to him belong;
They are weak, but he is strong.
Yes, Jesus loves me,
Yes, Jesus loves me,
Yes, Jesus loves me,
The Bible tells me so.

—W. B. Bradbury

I am so glad that our Father in heaven
Tells of his love in the Book he has given;
Wonderful things in the Bible I see,
This is the dearest, that Jesus loves me.
I am so glad that Jesus loves me,
Jesus loves me, Jesus loves me,
I am so glad that Jesus loves me,
Jesus loves even me.

—P. P. Bliss

God sees the little sparrow fall,
It meets his tender view;
If God so loves the little birds,
I know he loves me too.
He loves me too, he loves me too,
I know he loves me too;
Because he loves the little things,
I know he loves me too.

—Words by Maria Staub

School

It was hard for life for Riverview kids to be anything but wholesome. There was little around that wasn't good. Kids had no responsibilities. They were what parents were raising, and parents did most things for them. Kids were protected from practically everything.

Susan Struthers was a short vivacious girl with dark auburn hair worn short. She had a pointed nose, bright brown eyes, freckles and an outgoing personality. Barbara Kaye was blond with blue eyes, and wore her short hair cut bluntly all the way around, pulled to the side in front with a bobby pin. I had brown hair and green eyes and was taller than Barb or Sue. Frances Carson, being a year older, was the tallest of all. She was a year ahead of us in school, so we didn't start out with her. She was a dark-haired, shy girl, artistically talented like her father and mother. Her two front teeth were very white, and her eyes were black and bright. When in grade two Fran had a run-in with a teacher who broke a ruler over her back, her mother pulled her out of school for a year. The teacher was replaced. So by grade three all four of us were in the same class together and continued to be until grade eleven.

Life for us centred on Riverview School in the middle of the area, at the corner of Maplewood and Casey. It took almost twenty minutes to walk there and back from most points in the district. Since Barb, Sue, Fran and I all lived near one another, we always walked to and from school together, picking each other up as we went. In winter our moms would wrap scarves around our foreheads and over our noses, and we'd head out into the bitter north wind, clenching our fists inside our mittens to keep our hands warm, hurrying to get to school before we froze.

Built in 1908, Riverview was at first a small frame school with six grades (later nine) and a kindergarten. The radiators knocked from the steam heat and gave off a funny smell; the floors were made of narrow worn hardwood boards that went up and down. In the basement was the "auditorium" with a stage at one end; its long wooden benches with backs were moved into rows by the boys for assemblies. This was where school teas were held, TB X-rays taken, sex education films and other movies shown and physical training (PT) classes held. Later a brick addition was built on to the frame building to house the growing student population.

The principal of the school was Carson Abercrombie, a gentle grey-haired man who wore dark pinstriped suits. Almost all the teachers were spinsters, perhaps because of the absence of the men during the war. Most of the teachers wore their netted hair rolled in tight curls around the side. They wore skirts and blouses with cardigan sweaters over them, and oxfords or British Brevitts. Each teacher stayed in her room with her class from September till June, like a mother, and thus increased the sense of security in her pupils. Each teacher represented a grade, and had a certain reputation with the students, so you sort of knew in advance what the next grade was going to be like.

The little boys wore plaid flannelette shirts under pullover sweaters, the kind with reindeers or bears woven in patterns on them; they wore breeks held up with suspenders, and knee-socks, like Mounties. The girls wore oxfords, lisle stockings held up with garter belts and plaid skirts and sweaters. In Winnipeg public schools, though, girls were required to wear a uniform called a tunic. Tunics were navy blue serge with four block pleats in the front and four in the back, square necklines and no sleeves. They had belts whose two ends overlapped and buttoned with two buttons. There were two kinds of tunics, the real blue serge kind and the cheaper rayon kind that got shiny when pressed; the good ones cost about six dollars at Eaton's. Under the tunic, you wore a white blouse with short puffy sleeves or long sleeves; you wore long black stockings and blue cotton bloomers, known as blue pants. For everyday attendance, girls could wear a short-sleeved white blouse, or even a coloured one, but for formal occasions, such as school teas or choir performances, they had to wear long-sleeved white blouses with the sleeves rolled down and buttoned at the cuffs, collars buttoned at the neck and black ties. The uniform came from England, and its purpose was to equalize dress. But equality was the responsibility of only the girls; the boys could wear what they wanted. Tunics were a local tradition for many years and gave schoolgirls a satisfyingly scholarly appearance in public.

The classrooms had black slate blackboards and bulletin

boards above them where letters in the alphabet were written on white and green cards, examples of perfect penmanship. The desks were in rows, and had curly black iron frames; the desk of one attached to the seat of the next. The seats went up and down, and the desk tops had holes for inkwells on the right side. Light came in from a row of six large windows on the pupils' left. The teacher's desk was at the left side at the front of the room. At the back was a bulletin board and behind it the 'cloakroom' with hooks for the pupils' coats. Bad kids were made to go and stand in the cloakroom as punishment.

The teacher distributed foolscap or halfscap by giving it to the person in the front of each row who would pass it overhead to the person behind him, and so on all the way down. You ruled an inch margin down the side in pencil and wrote with a straight pen in a penholder, dipping it in the inkwell filled with washable blue ink supplied by the school. It was hard to write with a straight pen; often your nib would scratch, and fuzz from the paper would collect at the tip, making blotches on your work. You blotted everything after you wrote it with blotters supplied by the school. When you tried to erase something, you'd sometimes erase right through the paper. You had Dick and Jane readers and Think and Do workbooks. The teacher gave marks for spelling and arithmetic in percentages. Mistakes were called errors.

In school, the children were strictly regimented. There were several positions for sitting at a desk. Position one was with your hands clasped on the desk in front of you; position two with them straight out parallel; position three with your head resting on your arms, and so on. The teacher would command, Position one—TAKE! and you'd obey. In PT, of course, there were orders to stand at attention or at ease and to quick, march! Children were conditioned at an early age to obey or be punished. A tradition of stringent asceticism prevailed. There was a fifteen-minute recess twice a day after which children were recalled by a teacher ringing a hand bell, the signal for them to line up in allotted places on the sidewalk.

Riverview was a very intimate personal world. You moved from one grade to the next with your friends; the teacher changed, but you already knew who she was; your seat changed, but your classmates mostly stayed the same, as there was only one room for each grade. Little changed from one year to the next. Friendships begun in kindergarten were still intact in grade six and, with the children spending all day in the same room and walking to and from school together, became very tight.

The Great Flood

Nature in Winnipeg is nothing if not extreme. In the summer, it is extremely hot, with temperatures soaring to 100°. Tumbleweeds turn in the hot wind; there are pestilences of fish flies, mosquitoes, moths and army worms. Thunderstorms are violent and dramatic; they can be seen building up for miles on the horizon, huge mashed-potato storm clouds dragging blue veils of rain. There are hailstorms, and, on hot days, heat lightning. Sunsets are always a spectacle and always available to anyone who cares to look up—the sky is so big.

Winters are extremely cold, so cold that sometimes you don't go outside from one day to the next; people hibernate, or scurry from one oasis of warmth to the next. Sounds crackle and hiss, trees boom in the night. There are northern lights at night, and sundogs during the day, and when the weather's going to change, there's a circle around the moon. The amount of snow is tremendous. In 1955–56 we got a record ninety-nine inches. The snow is crystalline, pure and sparkly, its character constantly changing; sometimes it is hard enough to walk on; it piles up on roofs and fire hydrants in untouched mounds. Sometimes, the trees in the morning are laced with hoar-frost. Blizzards can stop the city's operation; in one, I remember, in November 1958, the only way to get downtown was to ski. The snow is heaped up all winter by big, efficient snowplows, until it forms ridges three or four feet high on each side of the street, and piles ten feet or so at each corner of an intersection.

Spring too is dramatic. The sun moves up from the south shining stronger and stronger on roofs, until the snow goes rotten and caves in, and the edges of shingles start to appear; three-foot icicles form, and there is dripping everywhere. Water starts running down the back lane, wearing channels through the grey ice and lying in deep puddles. The sign that spring has really arrived is the first robin, and the sound of heels going click click, instead of squeak squeak, down the sidewalk.

Every spring, before 1950, people watched the Red River with concern. They watched its flat snowy surface soften, split and break into thick ice floes that groaned and tried to climb over one another till the whole river started to move, sliding past the trees in slow white procession towards Lake Winnipeg. The ice floes, at first a mass, would become fewer and fewer as the weather got warmer, until only the occasional one would be coming down the river. Slowly the brown water would rise, usually overflowing its banks at the edges, and then drawing away, leaving the banks caked with cracking mud.

Although Churchill Drive ran all the way around Riverview, it was not high enough to protect the new houses, and every year people worried about the river. It had been high before, but it had never got out of hand. In the winter of 1950, though, there was more than the usual ninety inches of snow.

The ice broke up, and the river started to rise. It rose slowly, inch by inch, and in the usual human fashion, people assumed nothing would happen and did nothing. There were daily announcements of its height over the radio and in the papers. It rained. The river kept going up; its rise was insidiously uneventful. You couldn't see anything happening, the water didn't rush in torrents or foam or froth. It just lay there, brown, shining and threatening. People in the district volunteered to build dykes with sandbags, but after days of back-breaking toil on the dykes, they stood by helplessly as the flood waters bubbled up through the sewer holes which no one had thought to plug. The neighbours on Morley watched as one cautious family loaded all their possessions into a moving van and departed, even though the river was being contained by the dykes; a few days later, they were wishing they'd done the same, for by then, the houses on Morley were almost completely submerged. The main floors of the municipal hospitals were all under water, and the patients evacuated. Sidewalks floated away. People went up and down the streets in rowboats. The Riverview school auditorium was a swimming pool, with the upright piano floating around in it. From Casey Street on, the land rises, but the sewers backed up and all the basements were full of water. Jack Ellett's new restaurant at the corner of Baltimore Road and Osborne Street had eight feet of water in the basement.

For us kids, the flood was a lot of fun. It was like a big blizzard that disrupted the whole routine of adult life. You didn't have to go to school at all, because the school was full of water.

You walked down to Maplewood and Casey in your rubber boots and looked at it and laughed. It was just a bunch of water. You wanted to go rowing or get in on the action somehow, but your parents wouldn't let you, as the water was full of sewage, and there was risk of infection. But the parents didn't let the kids stand around and watch; Sue and I were sent to Neepawa for the month of May and missed all the fun. When we got back, everything was covered with mud. Houses showed mud halfway up the walls. Everyone's furniture and mattresses stood outside to dry. Everything was watermarked. The riverbank was just caked mud on top, and oozing slime underneath. In response, Churchill Drive was built up into a gravel dyke, protecting the whole district, and began to be known as the Dyke. The old pontoon bridge at the foot of Osborne Street was scrapped.

Friends

Ours was not the only group, by any means. Another group was formed by girls one grade ahead of us who lived on Ashland, Baltimore Road, Oakwood and Maplewood. They were older, cracked jokes, chewed gum and sometimes teased us on the way to school. They were scary. Like us, they picked each other up until by the time they reached school, they'd be strung out in a massed phalanx all across Casey. Yet another 'clique' was formed by girls living in the new postwar houses at the bottom of Ashland, Oakwood and Baltimore Road. They were bubbly, less academic, and popular with boys. Still another was formed by girls who had music in common. Most boys made their friends through playing hockey at the Community Club. The hard-core athletes formed one group, the bad boys from Lord Roberts formed another and the scholarly gentlemen formed their own small groups or kept to themselves.

Irene Holt lived in a new house at the bottom of Ashland directly across from the Riverview Community Club. Her friends were girls who lived around her in the other new postwar houses. Irene's dad, Russ, was scoutmaster at St. Alban's Anglican Church; consequently Irene was a Brownie and a Girl Guide, and her brother Ross a Cub and Scout. She had curly, reddish-brown hair and freckles, and when she laughed her eyes disappeared, so all that was visible under her thick dark brows were two crescents of dark eyelashes.

Terry Sim occupied a brick house with a green roof that overhung the front porch, on the northeast corner of Baltimore Road and Fisher, facing Fisher Park, a small elliptical park formerly known as Florence Park, between Ashland and Oakwood. Mr. Sim was an agent with Great West Life. Terry and her mom looked quite a bit alike; their oval faces, slanting eyes and longish noses gave them a vaguely feline quality. Terry's hair was black, but Mrs. Sim's had turned grey when she was still fairly young. Terry had her father's sloping shoulders, a diminutive upper torso, and legs like a ballet dancer's, with calves that were large in relation to her tiny feet. She was small, sparkly, dainty; her voice was airy and nasal. She liked horses and wanted to be a vet.

Maureen Butterworth's house was at the corner of Brandon and Hay streets. Her father was the business agent for the Federation of Civic Employers, and Maureen's great-grandmother, who lived to be 104 and had her picture published in the *Free Press,* was well known in Riverview. Maureen and her brother Tom, a lanky boy two years older than she, shared the Butterworth features—round eyes set fairly closely together and a long upper lip in a longish face—except Tom's was lean and Maureen's wasn't.

Janice Muirhead lived on Oakwood, just east of Fisher Park. Janice was the oldest of four children—herself, Margaret Ann, Brian and Patsy. Mr. Muirhead worked for Eaton's. The Muirheads were an organized and ambitious family, and all the kids received ample opportunity to develop the talents they possessed. Janice was very pretty and, like all the Muirheads, willow-slender; she had enormous blue eyes rimmed with dark lashes, a long and slender neck and a beautiful complexion. Janice had everything: she was quiet, down-to-earth, nice, and she had extraordinary co-ordination, which not only made her graceful and effortless in all sports, but also ensured that she played the piano and sewed very well. It all just seemed to come naturally.

Brenda Marshall, a tall, dark, intelligent girl, was the daughter of the Rev. George M. Marshall, who after being minister in Boissevain, Manitoba, became the new minister at Riverview United Church in 1950. The Marshalls lived in the manse on Baltimore Road. Brenda had two sisters, both younger, and all three girls had dark hair and dark eyes. Brenda started at Riverview in grade five, and since she played the piano very well, often played 'O Canada' and 'God Save the Queen' for assemblies and accompanied classroom choirs, as well as playing in a school orchestra. Being a minister's daughter and the eldest of three sisters gave her a maturity beyond her years, and she related more easily to adults than to kids her own age. Brenda was friends with us and with girls who played the piano and other instruments, like Karin Kozub, who played the cello.

Both boys and girls were friends with each other, as they continued through school together. Lionel Moore was friends with everybody. He was the son of Lionel Moore, a CBC radio announcer whose voice, heard daily at noon delivering the hog, sheep, grain and cattle prices, was as familiar an institution in Winnipeg as the Dominion Observatory Time Signal, and closely associated with it. Lionel Moore the elder had a shock of thick black hair, a homey unpretentious square face, and a relaxed open manner that communicated wholesome values. Mr. Moore was highly respected in Riverview. The Moores lived down past Fisher Park on Oakwood. The two Lionels were never known by anything so formal as senior and junior, just as Lionel and Lionel. Lionel had a younger brother Gerry, who was a good hockey player, and Lionel himself played hockey at the Community Club.

He was a skinny kid with narrow shoulders; his elasticized cotton pants were always in danger of either falling down or being pulled off. His short, light brown hair stood up in spikes at the front. His freckled face, with its heavy brow line, and wide mouth, usually wore an impish expression that went with Lionel's behaviour. He was a joker and a character. When his eyebrows furled down, he was laughing devilishly, enjoying a successful coup; when they went up, he was feigning innocence after somebody else got caught. His ability to pull deadpan expressions got countless other people into trouble.

Cliff Leach lived down the street in the same block on Balfour as my family. His father was a chartered accountant, and a warm handsome man. Cliff's mom was very pretty, with large blue eyes and a slender oval face, which Cliff inherited, along with his father's strong square jaw. Not only was Cliff goodlooking, but he got good marks and was good in sports. He was a heart-throb among the girls who lived in the new houses and of some of the other girls as well. He played hockey at the Community Club and made his friends among the athletes, who respected him, although he was studious, because of his ability in sports. He was quite shy and usually walked to school alone, likely to avoid the hordes of girls he might run into.

To the kids in Riverview, Lord Roberts territory was strange and alien; if Riverview was home, Lord Roberts was the Other. The streets were narrower, the houses closer together, it was dark and scary. We didn't know anybody from that side of Osborne Street, because they all went to Lord Roberts, and weren't part of our ambience. We had no opportunity to get to know them. In sports, of course, they were the enemy whom we had to beat. Their colours were the evil green, black and white, while ours were the righteous and familiar red and blue.

Lord Roberts school was a grey stone fortress with red trim around its windows; it even looked unfriendly. Its halls were strange. Lord Roberts boasted grades one to nine, while, at first,

Riverview had only grades one to six. The principal of Lord Roberts from 1943 to 1955 was Jack M. Scurfield, a big leonine man with reddish hair and bristling eyebrows. We knew of him, but had never seen him. Even in reputation he was terrifying, in comparison to our own innocuous Mr. Abercrombie in his linty pinstripe suits. The dark presence of Lord Roberts the Villain, lurking somewhere in the tulgy wood over there, a powerful big school full of kids who were just as competent as we were, made us feel innocent and defenceless by comparison, a sensation that was not entirely without basis in reality. If we thought the kids over there were bad and dangerous, they thought we were snobs and goody-goodies. When some of us went to Lord Roberts to take home economics, we hated it. It was so unfamiliar. And nobody knew who we were over there.

John Hodges was one connection between the worlds of Lord Roberts and Riverview. He lived on the corner of Montague and Osborne in a small white stucco house with dark red trim and a peak over the front door which faced kitty-corner out onto Osborne. His mother was a pretty, dark-haired woman, and his father a short, balding man who sold insurance.

John went to Lord Roberts, but came over to Riverview later. But even when he was going to Lord Roberts, his renown spread across Osborne Street. He was a Queen Scout at St. Alban's Anglican Church, under Mr. Holt's leadership, and sang angelically in a white choir gown in the St. Alban's choir. He was very good at sports and was catcher for a little league baseball team, which sometimes played at Riverview Community Club.

He was short, and dark and very goodlooking, with his mother's long eyelashes and bronze complexion, white teeth and regular features. His legs were slightly bowed. He was always precocious, got top marks in school, excelled at everything he did and always gave everything he had to whatever he was doing, particularly sports. He usually took the most responsible position in any team, that of catcher or goalie, with the most chance of getting hurt. And he got hurt—he had his nose broken twice and teeth knocked out, and his efforts to take it like a man wrung the hearts of spectators. John was regarded as more than just a plucky kid; he was a local hero.

John Kemp and Alan Ackland also bridged the gap between Riverview and Lord Roberts. Kemp lived on Arnold Avenue on the west side of Osborne. His father was a railroad man. He was very cute, his face exuding baby-faced charm, and always laughing. Alan Ackland, his buddy, was a tall, lanky rubbery boy with a dark brushcut. His grandmother babysat for many Riverview kids and knit them reams of mittens. Being from Lord Roberts, Kemp and Ackland were at first strangers to Riverview kids. They came over to play hockey, football and baseball at the Riverview Community Club. Although some of the Lord Roberts boys felt rejected by Riverview kids, and retaliated by regarding Riverview kids as goody-goodies, Kemp and Ackland gained acceptance easily by virtue of their athletic ability and their wit. Yet, there was always something independent about them; they could drop in and out of Riverview at will, like the lonesome cowboys in Park Theatre movies; they never had to belong. And neither of them was academically oriented, like most of the Lord Roberts bad boys. They came to Riverview to repeat grade nine.

Girl Guides

Outside of school, there were Brownies and Cubs, Guides and Scouts at St. Alban's Anglican Church one night a week. If you were a girl, first you went to Brownies, where you were a Pixie, or another type of fairy, and wore a brown uniform with a darker brown tie, a brown tam, a gold lanyard and earned brown badges with gold figures on them. Then you 'walked up' to Guides or, if you had earned your Golden Hand, 'flew up' in a ceremony which changed your status.

Sue, Barb, Irene Holt and I, as well as a number of the Lord Roberts girls, went to Guides in St. Alban's Church basement every Tuesday night. We lined up in our patrols in our blue cotton uniforms with green ties folded and doubled up the proper way, our white lanyards, our whistles, our belts with the Girl Guide symbol in the buckle and our navy blue tams. In front of us stood the company leader, Patricia Pinfold, as we raised our right hands, showing three fingers, and recited the threefold Guide Promise: 'I promise, on my honour, to do my best/To do my duty to God, the Queen and my country/To help other people at all times/To obey the Guide Laws.'

Then we recited, in unison, the Guide Laws:

A Guide's honour is to be trusted.
A Guide is loyal.
A Guide's duty is to be useful and to help others.
A Guide is a friend to all and a sister to every other Guide.
A Guide is courteous.
A Guide is kind to animals.
A Guide is obedient.
A Guide smiles and sings even under difficulty.
A Guide is thrifty.
A Guide is pure in thought, word and deed.

Then we would carry the colours, march around in single file, two abreast, four abreast, eight abreast, right wheel. We would break up into patrols and go into our patrol corners to practise knots—the reef knot, the clove hitch, the bowline, and so on, for our second-class and then our first-class badges.

Once we attained second-class status, we could get badges. We went around to different neighbours, who acted as judges for the badges. We did things we'd never otherwise have done: we groomed horses and cleaned stables for the horseman's badge; we made jams and jellies, cleaned ovens and sewed things for our homemaker's and sewing badges. The more badges you had, the better you were. Some girls from River Heights, glimpsed only on special occasions at Guide House on Roslyn Road, had badges all down their arms. At Guide House, we met Lady Baden-Powell (Bodden-Pole), Chief Guide, sent out from the centre of the Empire to visit the colonies, and couldn't understand her upper-class British accent.

Some of us only went to Guides to go to camp every year at Caddy Lake, where we camped in tents, cooked porridge and doughboys (pastry wound around a stick and roasted in the fire; you took the stick out and filled the hole with jam), swam, canoed and went on three-day overnight canoe trips through a series of tunnels, during which we subsisted on Gumpert's dried food. When the overnight canoes returned, the campers signalled to those on shore with their paddles, a moving sight. It was very romantic, sitting around campfires singing songs like:

> Land of the silver birch
> Home of the beaver
> Where still the mighty moose
> Wanders at will
> Blue lake and rocky shore
> I will return once more
> Boom tiddy waddy
> Boom tiddy waddy
> Boom tiddy waddy
> Boom.   —Words and music, John Cozens

Or getting up at seven in the misty morning and lining up to raise the colours, then going into the dining hall to a schottische played on the piano and singing all through porridge. At camp you could earn interesting badges—your Junior, Intermediate and Senior Red Cross swimming badges; your stalker's, for which you stalked the examiner through the bush so she couldn't hear you until you were upon her; your canoeist's, in which you had to dump a canoe and get it to shore; your woodcraft, where you wove a willow screen and dug a trench toilet; your astronomer's, where you identified constellations. We camped on a hill called Blueberry Hill, but were cautioned to disassociate it from the Fats Domino song of the same name.

But after a couple of years, even the overnight canoe trip wasn't enough to keep us interested in Guides. We were getting older, and boys were entering the scene.

Fun

C.E. Simonite's 250 new homes on the east side of Osborne Street were not built immediately, and for some time the acreage lay fallow. The vacant land where River Park had been became known as the Prairie. For kids it was full of mystery, with its little train tracks in the weeds, its overgrown foundations and old bear pits. We went there to fly kites, or with Mrs. Struthers to have a wiener roast on Sue's birthday; we rode our bikes on the sinuous paths which became known as the Monkey Trails, because of the monkey-tail way they snaked through the bushes. The ferris wheel seats stored there in the wooden shack, gathering cobwebs and dust were scary places to hide for hide and seek, and behind Mr. Ottensen's house was one of the miniature steam locomotives from the River Park train. The old bear pits and wolf dens still carried the taint of the animals they had housed, and one bear pit in particular was thought to have the bear still lurking within. The Prairie was scary. Strange men were said to lurk down by the river waiting to grab kids.

The old pontoon bridge was still in operation. In the winter, the hill at the foot of Osborne by the pontoon bridge made a tremendous toboggan ride. On Sunday afternoons you took your toboggan, and, dressed in your parka, toque, ski pants with leather patches on the knees and moccasins, you spent hours huffling and puffing up and down the hill until the snow clotted your pants and you couldn't feel your toes. It would grow dark, and soft snowflakes would fall past the one lone streetlight. When you got home with your bright red cheeks tinged with white patches of frostbite, your mom would sweep you off with a broom and give you some hot chocolate.

The Riverview Community Club boxcar was replaced with a new yellow stucco building in 1948, and the Lord Roberts boxcar was replaced by a similar yellow stucco building in 1950. Both community clubs had free-skating and hockey rinks with peewee, midget and Junior A and B hockey teams. At Riverview Community Club the boys played hockey and the girls fancy-skated; there was a loudspeaker that played the 'Skater's Waltz' and the 'Merry Widow Waltz'. None of the adults skated at all. We kids skated till our toes were numb; when we couldn't feel our toes any more, it was time to go in, loosen the laces and pound our feet a bit. Our fingers developed calluses from tying and untying laces. We walked to and from the skating rink on the wooden guards of our fancy skates, though some girls didn't wear the guards, so all the way up the sidewalk you could see, beside the treadmarks of snowplow tires, the marks of skate blades cut in the snow.

The Fort Rouge Yards still had their effect on the life in the district. Steam engines burned coal, puffed black smoke and housewives would discover their Monday morning washings flecked with soot and fly-ash. Blankets of black smoke that drifted over from the roundhouse often blotted out the sun on clear days. The black smog filled the subway so it looked like a dark cave. There was the chuffing of the steam engines all through the crystal nights, and on cold winter days, when sounds are especially penetrating, the noise of shunting box cars and coaches was carried over the neighbourhood. First there was a jarring crash, then a staccato banging until the coaches were coupled. There was the clanging of the steam engine's bells and the mournful sound of whistles. When the wind blew from the northwest, smoke from the smokestack blew over the district; you could tell the direction of the wind from the stack, and the time from the shop whistle. The noise was not at all offensive. It was a familiar, friendly noise; the solemn chuffings and bangings in the middle of the night were music to go to sleep by.

In the spring we skipped rope, shot aggies and played one, two, three alairy and seven ups against the school wall with our personal lacrosse balls. We rode our bikes and socialized on them. We played baseball with the boys at the corner of Ashland and Hay by the Struthers' house, with the sewer as home plate and the trees as bases. We played hide and seek in the Bush, the vacant lot across from Struthers'.

Fran, Sue, Barb and I remained friends out of school as well as in. We wore station wagon coats and angora Barbara Ann Scott bonnets with matching mittens knitted by our moms or their friends. We were sort of tomboys. In summer, we all had the same jackets, corduroy with link buckles at the front. Fran, the top dog, set the style with the first jacket, a dark red one, and the rest of us got them afterwards; Sue's was grey and mine was rust-coloured.

We wore those discouraging girl's jeans that zipped up the side, with wide legs and turned-up cuffs; on our feet were white socks and penny loafers.

Fran, Sue and I each had a dog. Each dog stood for its family. The Carsons' was an Irish Setter, called Rusty, who was sleek, beautifully coloured and quiet. Sue Struthers loved animals and wanted to be a vet; the Struthers' dog was an airedale called Monty, a tough rambunctious dog, wiry and energetic, like the war, somehow. The McCracken dog was a Springer Spaniel named Tucker, who was lovable and sweet. We took our dogs for walks in the Prairie. We bought chain collars and leashes for them, but mostly they ran loose. We tried to train them. We groomed them. We took pictures of them. But we didn't feed them; our mothers did that. We were always competing to see whose dog was best, and whose could swim the farthest into the Red River after a stick. Tucker was a non-competitive dog, and, when the other dogs jumped into the Red in pursuit, Tucker refused.

At home, we listened to our favourite radio programmes, and sometimes would go over to each other's houses to listen. During the Second World War, there were short-wave broadcasts that came over the radio from Britain, that faded in and out with a BBC voice riding in the centre of the static. People listened to the stand-up wooden radios the way they watch television now, except less passively. The radio programmes all came from the States—*Ozzie and Harriet, Fibber McGee and Molly, The Jack Benny Show* with Rochester, *Fred Allen, Amos and Andy, The Lone Ranger, Superman, The Black Museum, The Un-expecte-e-e-d.* After dinner on Sunday, we sat around in the dining-room listening to *Edgar Bergen and Charlie McCarthy,* or *Twenty Questions or Share the Wealth* ('Money Money Money Money—SHARE THE WEALTH!'). During the day there were soap operas, *Our Gal Sunday* and *Ma Perkins,* and at noon, *Bert Pearl and The Happy Gang,* with Kay Stokes at the organ. From *Amos and Andy,* the kids took their expressions—'holy mackerel, Kingfish', 'holy Moses', 'holy moley', 'holy murder', 'holy doodle', 'cripes', 'darn', 'heck' and 'goldarn', 'Damn', 'Christ', 'Jesus', 'Holy Jeesiz', and 'sonofabitch' were bad words; you could get your mouth washed out with soap if you used them.

We started out on A.A. Milne and the Burgess Bedtime Stories, by Thornton W. Burgess, which featured characters like Reddy Fox, Peter Cottontail, Poor Mrs. Quack, Buster Bear, Paddy the Beaver, Jerry Muskrat, and dramas set in the Green Forest and on the Green Meadow, or by the Laughing Brook or the Smiling Pond, with Old Mother West Wind looking on. When you walked in the Prairie and saw a meadow mouse, you assumed his name was Danny. We raced through the Bobbsey Twins Series by Laura Lee Hope, an American series featuring the Bobbsey Twins at the deep blue sea, the Bobbsey Twins at the circus, etc. The books we couldn't get at the Osborne Street Branch of the Winnipeg Public Library, such as the Nancy Drew Mystery Stories, featuring girl sleuth Nancy in a series of adventures *(The Secret of Red Gate Farm, The Mystery of the Ivory Charm)*, we saved our allowances for and bought at Eaton's for $1.37 each. We traded them around, until we'd read the whole series. Our moms subscribed to magazines for us—*Wee Wonder* and *Jack and Jill* and the *Children's Digest*, which had green-tinted pages to be easy on the eyes. We read about Uncle Wiggly, a rabbit, going out into the world to seek his fortune, and the Uncle Remus stories, with Bre'er Rabbit and Tarbaby and adventures in the Briar Patch; we read *Winnie the Pooh* and the usual fairy tales—*Cinderella, Snow White and the Seven Dwarfs, Sleeping Beauty* and the scary stories of Hans Christian Andersen.

In the library we discovered Albert Payson Terhune's books on valiant collie dogs—*Lad of Sunnybank, Bruce* (how a superb collie who turned from an ugly duckling into the pride of his owners repaid his friends' devotion by saving life and honour); *Treve* (a golden tawny collie in a large sheep ranch who risked his life to protect the sheep from rustlers and wolves); *Wolf* (the son of two beautiful champions, Wolf's clumsiness made him a nuisance but he gave his own life to save another). These stories attributed to dogs dignity and courage, and gave us new respect for our own pets, whom of course we romanticized accordingly.

We got horse-crazy, reading books like *The Black Stallion, Son of the Black Stallion, The Dark Horse* and *Hambletonian*, which was all about harness racing and its history in Kentucky blue grass country. There just weren't enough of those books. We took riding lessons together at the Tuxedo Riding Stables, a run-down operation in the bush south of Tuxedo, operated by a red-faced alcoholic named Johnny McLeod. Here we rode horses with names like Freckles and Vicky and Tex, and groomed their dusty behinds, pretending we were cowboys. Terry Sim also hung out at the Tuxedo Stables. Terry didn't get along well with her parents, and rejected them in favour of horses. She was much more horse-crazy than we were. For riding she wore a short brown cotton jacket with jeans. The jacket became Terry's trademark. Terry was also interested in art, and she had the first *Mad* magazines around. We used to go down and borrow them from her, and sit in the pine trees in Fisher Park reading the horror comics we weren't allowed to buy ourselves.

Comic books were a major influence on our impressionable young minds. The very first colour comic book after the war came out in 1946; called *Looney Toons and Merrie Melodies,* it had a picture of Porky Pig on the front. There were several series of comic books. The Warner Brothers group had Bugs Bunny, Daffy Duck, Sylvester the Pussycat and Tweety Bird ('I tought I taw a puddytat a-cweeping up on me/I did! I taw a puddytat, as pwain as he could be!'), Elmer Fudd and Mary Jane and Sniffles ('Magic words of poof poof piffles; make me just as small as Sniffles'); the Walt Disney series had Donald Duck and his three nephews Huey, Dewey and Louie waging their exploits with miserly old Unca Scrooge McDuck, who rolled in his rooms full of money and financed weird expeditions to Atlantis; it featured the mad inventor Gyro Gearloose, Mickey Mouse and Minnie, Goofy and Pluto. A lot of imagination went into the creation of these stories, as the Disney Studios were waxing to their peak, and the stories came alive on the pages. There were Tom and Jerry comic books, and Little Lulu was especially close to us; stories of her and Tubby and Witch Hazel and the Beebleberries were just crazy. There were Tarzan comics, featuring Jane and the chimp Cheetah; Roy Rogers comic books; Trigger comic books ('Whuhuhuho'); Champion the Wonder Dog comic books; Gene Autry comic books; Lone Ranger and Tonto comic books ('AIEEEEE!' cried the Indian as he got a bullet in the back); and those more obligatory Classics Illustrated comics.

Osborne Street was known locally as the Top; the bottom, which was not called such, was where the Community Club was, usually referred to as the Club. But, since all the shops and stores were on Osborne, when you were going to buy something, you said you were going 'up to the Top', as in up to the top of the street. The Top was our connection with the rest of Winnipeg, and going up to it was sort of like surfacing, up from the district into the city. The establishments at the Top purveyed their pleasures and illusions, tempting the pennies from our pockets with magical things we couldn't get at home.

In 1946, Mr. Juby sold the Rosedale Pharmacy to David R. Campbell, a slender, dark-haired crisp-looking man who had served in the navy in the war and who lived in the area on Churchill Drive. Mr. Campbell continued to operate the store as the Rosedale Pharmacy, but it became known as Campbell's Drugstore. Campbell's was 'the good' drugstore, identified in our minds with

Snow White and other heroines and heroes. Johnson's Drugstore, at the corner of Rathgar and Osborne and run by Mr. Johnson, who looked like Rudy Vallee with glasses, was, if not exactly the enemy, not so good. Campbell's had a high embossed metal ceiling with neon lights that hung down on chains, and the cabinets around the prescription counter at the back were dark varnished wood with glass doors. Mr. Campbell looked like a doctor in his short-sleeved white tunic with buttons down the side, and the drugstore was always orderly and friendly. Laurie Johnson, a pharmacy grad, joined Campbell's in 1950.

Campbell's was where we bought all our comic books. We went and got the latest one off the rack at the front of the store as soon as it came out at the beginning of the month. Most comic books were ten cents, except for Classics Illustrated, which were fifteen. Campbell's comic books were mostly of the innocent variety; there were a few horror and war comics, but, after a public outcry against war comics, they stopped. We also bought our Fudgsicles, Popsicles and Revels there.

The other main source of sweets and penny candy in the neighbourhood was Kozy Korner. It was operated by the Kozubs, who had previously run a small restaurant on Osborne Street when River Park was still open. There were five Kozub children, and the family lived behind the store.

Kids who lived in Riverview and Lord Roberts kids scraped together their pennies or a couple of pop bottles and cashed them in for goodies. Kozy Korner had a wide selection—blackballs, licorice pipes and twisters, jellybeans and jujubes, lollypops and large pinwheel all-day suckers. In the freezer there was a cardboard tube of ice cream on a stick with red and white stripes around it like a barber pole, and you pushed the ice cream up through the tube to eat it; there were soldier boys and dixie cups and prepacked ice cream cones covered with nuts called drumsticks costing ten cents, while the others were six cents. There were two kinds of bubble gum, the coloured balls sold in a glass dispenser for a penny, and Dubble Bubble, the gum that made better bubbles and came with a comic strip inside the wrapper, for two cents. Kozy Korner was viewed as a suspicious and conspicuously ethnic encampment by the predominantly Anglo-Saxon enclave of Riverview. Because the Kozubs were foreign, they were first associated with the influx of Displaced Persons into the neighbourhood after the war, children in babushkas to whom one was kind and understanding. And later, in the fifties, it was rumoured that Mr. Kozub, by virtue of his Slavic origins, was a communist.

Anybody who let his sentimentality show by naming his store Kozy Korner must be suspect.

In imitation of these confectioners, who loomed large in our lives, we kids set up sidewalk stands and sold Freshie for two cents a glass.

The Park Theatre, of course, was *the* major attraction at the Top. Movies satisfied our imaginations with less work than it took to read a book; you could just sit there and bask in pleasure. Fran, Sue, Barb and I had a club. We called ourselves the Green Hornets. We were going to make identical capes for our club, though we never got around to it. We relied instead on our corduroy jackets for our identity. Our club went to the Park every Friday night. Since there was no concession in the theatre, we'd each buy a chocolate bar at Campbell's before going in. We bought our tickets, green admission tickets torn off a roll, for twenty-five cents from Mrs. Besler, who sat behind the ticket window. Inside Mr. Besler, with his grey suit, round black-rimmed glasses and broad beaming face, would tear them in half.

There we could see all our favourite characters—Donald Duck, Mickey Mouse, Woody Woodpecker, Bugs Bunny, Tom and Jerry, Daffy Duck, Sylvester and Tweety—come alive on the screen; the cartoons were even better than the comic books. There was usually a black and white news short, which ended with a movie camera turning slowly towards the audience, military music and the words 'The Eyes and Ears of the World'. The music changed with every item, and often the news was as old as the second-run movies we saw.

It was at the Park that we became acquainted with the lovable MGM lion, with the torch-bearing lady from Universal, with the J. Arthur Rank muscleman and his gong and the Twentieth Century Fox searchlights. We knew absolutely nothing about New York or Hollywood or the Bronx or the American West, except what we saw at the Park; as far as we were concerned, these places didn't exist in the real world; they existed only in the movies at the Park. The movies were very personal to us. The characters who talked funny and acted funny were familiar parts of our lives, and we felt they were friends. The Bowery Boys, Louie, and Satch in his baseball cap, were from the Bronx, but we didn't know it. Even Bugs Bunny talked in a New York accent, but we didn't recognize it for that. The Three Stooges, Laurel and Hardy and the Marx Brothers were just funny guys who made us laugh.

Jungle movies were big. At first Johnny Weissmuller played Tarzan; he could swim in the river as fast as Jane ran along the riverbank. When Weissmuller got too fat, Lex Barker played Tarzan; he was the Tarzan in the comic books, but somehow the comics were better. Johnny Weissmuller became Jungle Jim, a white hunter in a big hat with a leopard-skin band on it. There was Frank Buck and *Bring 'Em Back Alive,* and Bomba the Jungle Boy, in his loincloth and curly blond hair. The war-cry of our club was Johnny Weissmuller's 'Ah-eeah-eeah-eeah', and favourite expressions were 'Kreegah Bundolah' and 'Ungawa' which is actually Swahili for 'let's get outa here'.

Cowboy movies were also important. Kids played cowboys and Indians and had cap guns and holsters and twirled lariats. The Roy Rogers movies were in Trucolor and always a different colour from other movies. There were Roy, Dale, Trigger, Andy Devine, Pat Brady in his jeep, Nellybelle, and the Riders of the Purple Sage, singing 'Along the Navajo Trail'. Everybody at Roy's Double R. Bar ranch was a singer. There were also movies with Hopalong Cassidy and his white horse Topper. There were westerns with Randolph Scott, who was sort of a responsible hero, with James Stewart, John Wayne, Robert Taylor and Audie Murphy. Of course we had our favourite cowboy actors, but we liked the horses more than the cowboys; nothing could top a movie about a wild stallion fighting for his freedom.

There were adventure movies—Errol Flynn in swordfight and pirate movies, Burt Lancaster in *The Flame and the Arrow* or *Apache,* Stewart Granger in *The Wild North* and *Scaramouche.* We meditated on these men; I saw one Errol Flynn movie five times. There were lots of films of Broadway musicals—*Porgy and Bess, Showboat, Oklahoma!, Guys and Dolls, Carousel, Annie Get Your Gun,* with Betty Hutton, *Calamity Jane,* with Doris Day and Howard Keel, *My Fair Lady,* with Julie Andrews and Rex Harrison— all full of beautiful women actresses with ringlets, tight corsets, low necklines and big skirts. People breaking into song in the middle of the dialogue we thought kind of corny.

Then there were movies our parents might see too—*Lassie Come Home, The Wizard of Oz, National Velvet,* with Elizabeth Taylor, *My Friend Flicka.* A Walt Disney movie, such as *Snow White and the Seven Dwarfs* or *Bambi,* was a major event. The films seemed to reach their peak with *Cinderella.*

The scariest movie ever to play at the Park was the original *One Million B.C.,* where everybody sat around in caves gnawing on flesh, while bood pumped rhythmically from the throats of expiring dinosaurs and boiling hot lava suffocated one and all. Quicksand was the grabber; any movie featuring that usually had you under your seat, and the Hollywood studios really wrung those quicksand scenes out.

Times were changing, and by 1949 or 1950 a new optimism began to manifest itself in small ways in the district. Wartime associations began to be forgotten, and people began to believe that life was going to be more than marginal. There was enough faith in the future to keep building.

The Park Alleys, an eight-lane, five-pin bowling alley owned by Ray Bradshaw (also an area resident), was built in 1949, as an additional attraction at the Top. A pink stucco building with a modern overhang, and large solid blue tin letters hanging from it spelling its name, Park Alleys had in its front façade a rectangular and a diamond-shaped glass-brick window. Glass bricks looked modern, and were advertised a lot at the time as being cheaper than windows because they required no frames, but they had the disadvantage of leaking. David Campbell also added a panel of glass bricks in the Beresford window of his drugstore. Boxy brick apartment blocks three storeys high went up between Bartlett and Oakwood on Osborne, with decorative strips of glass bricks in the sides. Squat white stucco apartments filled up the vacant lots at Clare and Osborne and Balfour and Osborne, in some cases with glass bricks over the doors. The Jewel grocery store near Jubilee and Osborne opposite Balfour had a front of black vitrelite, another sexy new material.

Another postwar addition to Osborne Street was a new restaurant, built in 1950 by Jack Ellett who lived on Churchill Drive. Ellett's restaurant was just what the Top needed to complete the scene. A small low building with a fieldstone front and a modernistic curved overhang, Ellett's, with its gay red and white scalloped awning, tempted us with visions of candy, sweets and fun. Mr. Ellett sold the neighbourhood kids on goodies we couldn't get at home—French fries, hamburgers, milkshakes, floats and sodas. When he first opened the restaurant, his specialty was thirteen-inch hot dogs in foot-long buns, fresh up from the States. The restaurant had three long tables with cream arborite tops, each with six swivel stools. In the main area were two U-shaped counters surrounded by swivel stools and a long counter at the back. Mr. Ellett later added cushy white Hollywood-style booths. The walls were pale green, and up above were red and white stripes.

On the counters were serviette containers, straw holders, and salt and pepper shakers, grouped around small juke box extensions whose panels you could turn with a handle to choose three songs for a quarter. Behind the counter were banks of stainless steel, with milkshake machines, rows of flavour compressors, ice cream freezers, French fry cookers, hamburger grills, milk dispensers. Ellett's was a model display of American soda fountain technology, which was brand new to us. It held a lot of power and mystery for us whose mothers would scarcely allow us to have a soft drink. The ice cream at home came in square slabs cut off bricks; Mr. Ellett's came in scoops. The potatoes at home were mashed; Mr. Ellett's were cut into French fries. You couldn't get hamburgers at home at all.

We were always finding excuses to go over to Ellett's and we used Ellett's against our parents. Mr. Ellett started making honey donuts, twenty-five dozen a day, and sold them in boxes at the front corner to lure us over. Pretty soon, smart moms started making hamburgers for lunch, and dads found themselves stopping off at Ellett's on the way home for a box of honey donuts. With the advent of soft ice cream, Mr. Ellett spent $700 on an outside sign and $3000 on a soft ice cream machine. He and his son Barry, in their white shirts, did a rousing business for a while. But when the Dairy Queen opened above Brandon Avenue in 1954, Mr. Ellett's soft ice cream cones lost out in authenticity; kids started to walk all the way up to the DQ for the original cone with the curl on top.

We viewed Mr. Ellett in the same light as we viewed Mr. Carson. His work was fun, a kind of showbusiness, he had all this great fascinating equipment we could watch the waitresses using as we cra-a-cked our milkshakes to the last drop. He was good, like Walt Disney, on the kids' side, and he was kind of exotic and mysterious. He stood for another way of life. Those who had any connection with America—Mr. Besler, Mr. Carson, Mr. Ellett—had power in our eyes, and were more interesting than our staid parents because they were associated with fun and pleasure; and they still managed to make money at it. In our parents' view, work was work, and pleasure was immoral; anybody who made money out of selling pleasure was in their eyes a bit suspicious.

Across the street from Ellett's was the alternate hangout, the Riverview ice cream shop, two doors away from Campbell's. It was known as Greeves. It was a little bake-shoppy kind of place, with pastries and things in the front window. At a little counter girls in starched white smocks would dig out ice cream cones with scoops from under stainless steel lids. You could get hot dogs and chips there too. And at the back were about four booths, two on each side. They had things like mocha cake and date squares; it was sort of a bakery with hamburgers.

There was nothing wrong with Greeves; it was not a dive or a joint, it was every bit as respectable as Ellett's. But whereas Ellett's on the east side of Osborne Street was patronized mostly by Riverview kids, Lord Roberts kids hung out at Greeves on the west side. Greeves was said by the parents of Riverview kids to be a 'hangout' and therefore bad.

Since Ellett's and Campbell's Drugstore and the Park were such important parts of our lives, we took an intense interest in any changes that were made, as it affected us almost more than it affected the owner. Ellett's was sacred, our own emporium of exotica, a refuge from our parents, as were the Park and Campbell's. We viewed the slightest change with dismay; no improvement was as good as letting things stay the same, for in our eyes change always hurt, and things were always better before.

Music

Many of the girls in the district took piano lessons, among them Janice, Brenda and I. There were two piano teachers in the district. Miss Derby inhabited a huge red brick mausoleum of a house on Baltimore Road; she was an older, homely spinster. Claire Howard, who lived in the house right opposite the school at Maplewood and Casey, was young, blond and charming. They charged $1.25 for a weekly lesson.

Piano lessons were a refinement and hopefully an initiation into the rigorous academic tradition of music in Winnipeg. Music is very important in Winnipeg and always has been closely associated with church and school. Playing the piano was promoted by moms as something you could do all your life and enjoy. So, reluctantly bidding goodbye the day beckoning outside, you'd take your music dictation book, your sheet music and the Royal Conservatory of Toronto or University of Manitoba book of test pieces in a zip-around briefcase, and go once a week for your lesson. You'd sit in the teacher's waiting room after four until the previous pupil was finished. You would go in and sit on the piano stool, spinning it till it was low enough for your feet to reach the pedals. The teacher would sit in a chair beside you, and listen to you first play your major, minor and melodic scales, your major and minor chords, solid and broken, and your arpeggios. You would play your pieces, which had names like 'Lullaby' or 'Little Bo-Peep' or 'The Yellow Butterfly' for her; you had to learn a Bach two-part invention and a Mozart sonatina. With your teacher, you selected your test pieces for your next examination in September. You practised those same pieces for nine months until the exam. On the books you had there were names like Hanon and Czerny, Healey Willan and Scribner.

You were initiated into the world of stout, long-haired romantic and classical composers with surly faces, men dressed in funny coats with stand-up collars and cravates. The music was taught in a rigid pattern; first the scales, chords and arpeggios, in a different key signature each week. Then the Bach, then the Mozart, then a romantic piece and finally an impressionist; the impressionist always came last because he was the most recent, and still a little suspect. The same pattern went on for years and years.

By grade six, you were supposed to practise two hours a day, and while you were in there plodding through your same old pieces once again, you could hear other kids out on the street playing baseball or riding their bikes. It was embarrassing too, because people knew you were supposed to be able to play the piano, but when they asked you to play something, all you could play were your test pieces, and you were so nervous about them, because they'd assumed such tremendous importance in your mind, that you would forget them half the way through. In desperation, some of us went out and bought sheet music of 'The Bumble Boogie' or something that *we* wanted to learn that wasn't imposed on us, to find out if we really could play the piano. But you received no support for this, as popular music was frowned upon.

The first Manitoba Musical Competition Festival was held on May 13 and 15, 1919, in Grace United Church. It was organized by the Men's Music Club, which was formed from groups of people who sang together and played gramophone records together at each other's homes. This club was at first a male voice choir and then a philharmonic choir, and soon became the main source of serious music in the city, finally forming the Winnipeg Symphony. The Men's Music Club brought in guest conductors until the Gees, a local family of impresarios, took over with their Celebrity Concert Series in the thirties and forties.

For the festival, which was based on the British tradition of music festivals, the club imported four or five British adjudicators to judge the competitions.

The adjudicators were distinguished musicians who had had important experience in English festivals. For instance, Hugh Roberton, the composer of 'Dream Angus', adjudicated at Winnipeg. The participants in the postwar years numbered about 14,000 or 15,000 annually. The British adjudicators who have graced the Canadian festivals are the product of the festival movement in the British Isles, of which the British Federation of Musical Competition Festivals is the co-ordinating central body. The Federation was incorporated by Act of Parliament on November 10, 1921, and the Manitoba Festival was the first Canadian festival to become its affiliate, the certificate of membership being dated June 26, 1922. There are 200 festivals co-ordinated by the Federation. The Festival usually had 300 or 350 choirs. A child who went to school in Winnipeg could scarcely miss being in the Festival. Its serious, British, attractively academic atmosphere hung in the air all year.

This annual raising of childish voices and the rippling of piano music started at the same time the snow melted and gurgled down back lanes, and the robins returned. For months during the winter, thousands of eager piping voices had been led through the test pieces by conductors, usually teachers, each pushing their brood through the piece with effusive gestures and facial gyrations. Each classroom choir or larger choir had learned the test piece and one song of its own choosing; the test piece had been practised and practised over and over again, till every note, every phrase, every catch of breath had been engraved on every little memory. The kids who couldn't carry the tune were allowed to stand in the choir and mouth the words without singing; they were called goldfish.

Outside the classroom, kids who took music lessons practised their own test pieces diligently. It could be a piece from the exam book, so the kid wouldn't waste any effort learning anything extra. People who wondered why he was practising so hard were told in whispers that he was entering the Festival this year. The Festival was the most refined form of competitive torture ever devised for kids.

The day the choir was to perform was of course a day off from school. Kids would come to school squeaky clean, their hair shining, the runs in the girls' black stockings sewn up, the sleeves of their white shirts rolled down and buttoned, their ties neatly tied and their tunics pressed. The boys' hair was slicked down with water; they wore white shirts with ties. They would pour into the orange Festival buses and sing all the way down to the Civic Auditorium, at the corner of Memorial Boulevard and St. Mary's Road, behind The Bay. The buses pulled up at the side of the auditorium, and disgorged their cargo of chattering girls, who were arranged in lines by the nervous teacher, dressed in her best suit, with a corsage of flowers, presented to her by the choir, pinned to the lapel. The files, mainly of girls, moved slowly into the building, past the glass cases containing stuffed buffalo, Indians in buckskin and feathers, squaws, papooses, tomahawks, teepees, bows and arrows (the auditorium used to be Winnipeg's museum)—and into the hall itself.

The auditorium, home of the Winnipeg Symphony, bore the city's Manitoba buffalo crest and motto—'Commerce, Prudence and Industry'—on a banner above the stage. The main floor was flat and filled with dark rows of wooden chairs with fold-up seats, divided into a centre section, with two sets of seats down either side. Above them, the balcony seats ringed the room in a giant U. Towards the front in the centre section was a table; here sat the adjudicator, with his notebook and his teacher's desk bell, the kind you tap on top to make a discreet ding for attention.

The girls and boys moved down into the building, glancing nervously at the other choirs already seated. They moved into their section and took their seats with great clangings and clatterings, a little self-conscious before the competition's eyes. This was an occasion where school spirit came to the fore. The girls took off their coats and looked around, craning their necks in all directions, and combed their hair all over again. The floor of the auditorium was now a mass of black and white; everywhere shiny hair was being preened with great show.

Meanwhile, elsewhere in the city, in some barren cold church hall, the top of the Heintzman grand stood expectantly open. A mother in a seal coat and felt hat with feathers in it waited benignly beside her eight-year-old. He would be shaking in the seat beside her, dreading the moment his number would be called; when it was, he stumbled up to the stage, the bell dinged and he launched into 'The Yellow Butterfly'. The adjudicator, who had already heard the piece seventy-five times that afternoon, braced himself to try to distinguish this version from the others, so he could assign a mark. The young performer's family status in the community, his mother's worth as a mother, as well as the knowledge that the adjudicator had heard before what he was about to play, rode on his small shoulders. Consumed with nerves, he stumbled through the piece red-faced and dashed from the piano in a paroxysm of stage fright.

Now the announcer called over the PA system for 'Competitah Numbah 1', in an unmistakably British accent. A flurry started in one corner of the auditorium. The choir rose as one, snapping the fold-up seats back, pulling up stockings, straightening tunic pleats, taking out chewing gum and sticking it to the undersides of the seats. The choir filed, row by row, layer by layer, like black and white wool unravelling, up the aisle, up the stairs onto the stage, shortest in front, tallest in back, the front row walking all the way across and the teacher in front gesturing where to stop. The other rows filed in behind, until the choir was a solid block of faces above white blouses and black tunics. The teacher arranged her group just so, moving them a little bit to the left, then to the right. Her back to the audience, she folded her hands in front of her. Suddenly the choir burst into laughter; the teacher had made a funny face to get them relaxed. No extraneous touches, such as uniforms that differed from the norm or imaginative ways of getting on and off the stage, were tolerated; nothing but the musical performance was allowed to influence the adjudicator.

The accompanist, also with a corsage, a student or another teacher, moved to the piano and opened her music. The auditorium became silent; all eyes were on the group on stage, watching beadily for the slightest slip. It was like a command performance, the British tradition was everywhere—in the music, the uniforms, the adjudicator and the accents. The teacher poised on the tips of her Brevitts, her hands folded on her solar plexus, smiled over her choir, awaiting the signal. The spidery hand of the adjudicator came down on the bell, and the ding broke the silence like a diamond tossed into a well.

The teacher spread her arms over the choir, and then mouthing one, two, she launched her group into the song, cutting the air with her hands in her own special way to keep time, sometimes with elaborate gyrations, sometimes with a minimal gesture. In a pianissimo part, the teacher crouched down, exhorting her group to be mouselike, all the while pronouncing the words soundlessly, stretching her mouth every which way. When a crescendo rose, the teacher waved her arms, like a rooted tree tossed in a storm, to pull the best from her choir. It was her finest hour. The voices soared pure and flute-like; the children gave what she asked of them; changing for a moment from little brats into perfect angels. Clear high notes soared breathtakingly, British accents in British songs:

When Cats Run Home—Words by Alfred Lord Tennyson
Music by Herbert N. Howells
Copyright 1911 by Novello &
Co. Ltd.

When cats run home and light is come,
And dew is cold upon the ground,
And the far-off stream is dumb,
And the whirring sail goes round,
And the whirring sail goes round,
Alone and warming his five wits,
The white owl in the belfry sits.

When merry milkmaids clock the latch,
And rarely smells the new-mown hay,

And the cock hath sung beneath the thatch,
Twice or thrice his roundelay,
Twice or thrice his roundelay,
Alone and warming his five wits,
The white owl in the belfry sits.

The Lincolnshire Poacher—Folk song arranged with
descant by H. A. Chambers

As me and my companions
Were setting of a snare,
Twas then we saw the gamekeeper,
For him we did not care;
For we can wrestle and fight, my boys,
And jump out anywhere.
Oh, tis my delight, in the season of the year,
Yes, tis my delight of a shiny night,
In the season of the year.

Dream Angus—Gaelic air from Pictures in Song
Arranged by Hugh S. Roberton

Mm . . . Mm . . . Mm . . .
Can ye no hush yer weepin', O?
A' the wee lambs are sleepin', O,
Birdies are nestlin', nestlin' thegither,
Dream Angus is hirplin owre the heather.

List to the curlew cryin', O.
Fainter the echoes dyin', O,
Even the birds and beasties are sleepin',
But my bonnie bairn is weepin', weepin'.

Dreams to sell, fine dreams to sell;
Angus is here wi' dreams to sell,
Hush ye, my baby, and sleep without fear;
Dream Angus has brought you a dream, my dear.
Mm . . . Mm . . . Mm . . . Mm . . .

Sure, the singing was thrilling. Sure, the performances often
reached astonishing heights of purity and perfection. But then the
song dropped away to nothing. For a moment the hall was still,
then applause swelled like static in the auditorium. The choir
unravelled and flowed back off the platform, and became just
schoolkids again. The choir director, flushed and excited, tried to

conceal it from her choir. The audience consulted its programme, and the process was repeated. The British voice called for 'Competitah Numbah 2', and another section of the auditorium rose en masse.

When the last choir had performed, and the gum had been peeled from the undersides of seats and put back in mouths, an expectant hush fell over the auditorium. After a few moments, the adjudicator himself, bearing his verdict in a book or clipboard, slowly mounted the stairs to the platform. He was often a hook-nosed professorial type with baggy trousers, jacket pockets bulging with notes, round, wire-rimmed glasses and hair sticking out in some eminently British way. Everybody in the hall loved him at this moment, and applause burst from all sides; everybody wanted to win and maybe giving him lots of applause would help. Mothers and friends watched from the balcony. The applause quickly subsided. He went to the microphone and began speaking, often in such a thick accent he was difficult to understand. Stating what he expected from the test piece, he then went over each choir in detail, pointing out faults of interpretation, tonality, phrasing, tempo, etc., doling out a bit of praise here, a bit of criticism there, tossing in the odd joke. The audience was restless. Finally he came to the end: 'The winnah is—Competitah Numbah 2!'

As his lips were seen to form the word 'two', wild screams erupted from the victorious section. The choir director lost her self-possession and hugged the accompanist. The other choirs, too dazed to make any noise, finally filed out sorrowfully. The auditorium emptied quickly, and the choristers rushed back to tussle and sing all the way home on the orange bus, as it bounced past the mounds of blackened lumpy snow, now the consistency of pastry on the sidewalks.

Speed Skating

Eventually Riverview School got a new principal, Mr. R.T.F. Thomson, a small man who wore grey suits and thinning grey hair and a bristly moustache. He spoke in a high voice, with a lisp. The onus was on him to give Riverview an identity as a junior high school. The sport he chose to give Riverview a reputation was speed skating.

Every year, at the Osborne Street Amphitheatre, a huge old creaky firetrap where the risk was so high that parents were afraid to take their children to the Shriners' Circus, the schools competed in city-wide skating races, one of the only authentically Canadian events that took place there. The amphitheatre housed shows like the Ice Cycles, and until the Winnipeg Arena was built in 1955, it served as a hockey rink. Winnipeg, of course, had no team in the NHL.

There was a lot of skating potential in Riverview that nobody had tapped. Cliff Leach was a good hockey player, and so was John Hodges, and many other boys—Brian Allen, Wayne Stewart, John Mansley—had spent a good part of their lives on skates. Among the girls, there was Janice Muirhead and her red-headed sister Margaret Ann, and lots of others—Jennifer Bell, Janeva Bailie—who had learned to skate at the Community Club on fancy skates on the free-skating rink.

Mr. Thomson took the matter in hand. He persuaded Fred Green, then president of the Community Club, to have a speed-skating rink flooded on the football field, and we began to train at lunch hour. Girls soon discovered they were terribly handicapped trying to chop corners in fancy skates, which was what most of the girls wore to compete in the races. Fancy skates were okay for three-jumps, rabbit hops, spirals, swans, the prayer, shoot-the-duck, sit spins, and trying to be Barbara Ann Scott, but were next to useless when it came to going fast. So Mr. Thomson suggested we ask our parents if they could afford to get us real speed skates, which we did. We went skating at noon instead of going home, and did laps around the track. What a thrill it was to use those skates. You could go much faster and glide much longer with one push. It was simple and graceful and exhilarating, going around in twenty-five below weather, inhaling the icy air, face in the biting wind. You swung your arms out behind you, and when you were cross-cutting the corners, you tucked one arm behind your back, let the other one swing and bent over as far as you could to cut the wind resistance. We felt very glamorous and professional.

Up to this time, Riverview School had had kind of an apologetic, ingratiating image. There was nothing to be proud of. So when we went to the amphitheatre in the winter of 1953, carrying our speed skates, wearing our red and blue sweaters, we had no idea what to expect. We had competed in grade school, but with no particular success. We didn't have much confidence. The schools turned out en masse, as usual, both skaters and cheering section. The races were divided under the height and weight categories of primary, junior intermediate and senior boys and girls, individual races and relays. The best skaters in the school would be ready, wearing their school sweaters, to carry their school colours to victory.

It was do or die. The races weren't very long, and there were a lot of them. The skaters would line up at the blue line and start with a gun. At the start of each race, screaming would break out—'Come on John! Come on, come on!'—and would rise to a pitch of hysteria as the skaters entered the final lap and crossed the finish line. Much to Riverview's surprise, no other school wore speed skates. Our hearts were in our mouths, and we were all screaming too, of course, as Brian Allen finished almost a lap ahead of the guy behind him. John Hodges left them all standing, and our hearts broke when Cliff Leach, chopping around a corner, stumbled, fell and skidded into the boards. But then he got up and crawled over the finish line on his hands and knees to win! We went wild when we learned that Riverview had taken top place in the city. From then on, we had a reputation.

We repeated the triumph next year. By this time, we were skating with a swagger. Speed skating had drawn a lot of interest in the neighbourhood, and had become the thing to be in. Mr. Thomson, in his brown mouton coat and fur hat, honoured all the practices with his presence, his breath steaming, his cheeks rosy in the air.

Leaving Junior High

We were changing. By the end of grade nine, Sue, Fran, Barb, Jan and I all had pixie cuts we'd made Sophie of Sophie's Hair Styling cut for us. The bangs were jagged like teeth all across the forehead, there were kiss curls at the sides. We wore circular skirts with crinolines, sweaters and medallions. We began to get pimples. Where did pimples come from? Why did we have them? Nobody knew. We squeezed them, fascinated; we had blackheads too. There was a new product called Clearasil that not only covered pimples up but medicated them at the same time. All of us wore it, and carried tubes of it around in our coat pockets. Our faces must have looked like mud-packs. The pimples still showed through.

Boys had joined us on the walks to and from school. Fran, Sue, Barb and I teamed up with John Malo, who lived on Montgomery and came from a French-Canadian family; he wore a corvette coat and was known as Butch because he wasn't very. When Mr. Martin instigated square-dancing in the school auditorium, Butch was the star dancer. Frenchie, John Mitchell, who lived near Butch and was also French Canadian, walked with us, as did John Hodges. Cliff still walked by himself, keeping his distance from the Gang. The boys started to throw us in the snow and to use us to try out the stepover toeholds and hammerlocks and half Nelsons and piledrivers they'd picked up from watching Whipper Billy Watson and Lord Athol Layton wrestle at Maple Leaf Gardens on TV. By the time we'd got home, we'd been smashed on the head by books, had our nylons torn, and had snow down the backs of our necks and red, tweaked ears; we loved every minute of it.

In 1955, at the end of grade nine, June graduation ceremonies for Riverview School were held at Riverview United Church. The boys wore sports jackets, bolo ties, drapes and pointy black shoes. They had begun to cultivate little waves that broke over their foreheads and to grease their hair. The girls wore flat ballerina shoes so as not to be taller than the boys, pastel dresses of princess design in dotted swiss or shiny cotton, approved of by moms, pearl or bead chokers and matching button earrings. It was a beautiful hot summer day. Reverend George Marshall presided. As valedictorian, I gave a shy two-minute speech read from a piece of paper. The choir sang 'Non Nobis Domine'. Cliff Leach was the man of the hour; he was already going steady with Linda Thorsteinson, a bubbly blond who lived in a new house on Balfour, and who was the most popular girl in the school. He wore his sports coat, drapes, pointy black shoes and bolo tie; she wore a semi-formal with a little bolero and high heels; her hair was styled in a 'bustle'. After the ceremony, they posed for a picture outside Riverview School. Everyone was proud. Mr. Muirhead took home movies. This graduation seemed kind of superfluous since we were only leaving junior high. But next year, a new high school was opening. And we would be its first class. Things would never be the same again.

III Teenage Life

The Climate

Up until the end of the Second World War, the dominant influence on South Fort Rouge Life had been the British Empire. On maps, Canada was one of the pink countries which belonged to the Empire, and then to the Commonwealth. As an ally in the war, Canada identified closely with Britain. In Winnipeg, British traditions were respected and valued: they were perpetuated in school ceremonies, the Festival, the traditions and values of the church, Girl Guides and Brownies. There were also little things which had been grafted onto small-town prairie life and gave it a veneer of Victorian respectability—oatmeal porridge in the morning, afternoon tea, fruit cake, well-done roast beef with Yorkshire pudding and lots of brown gravy on Sundays. Beneath this patina of English culture, the reality of Canadian life meant enduring harsh sunny winters in an outpost of the Empire. The people, many of whom had been born in the Old Country, clung to the old ways.

However, after the war, as American capital and culture poured into Canada, British influence on Canada gradually gave way to American influence. The Americans, of course, had had their influence on life everywhere much before that, with their industrial machines, their development of electricity, the telephone, the motor car, radios and aeroplanes. After the war, the prosperity that American growth and expansion brought to Canada allowed Canadians to participate in the American way of life: to progress was to acquire the new products coming up from the States. And to use them, people had to act in ways that were American, not British; suburbia was American and people who lived in a ranch-style bungalow couldn't help feeling a little bit American.

But that was okay, because everything American was so desirable. America appeared to be the source of all good things, things that were magical and ingenious and fun. The products that enticed us at the Top—Cokes, thirteen-inch hot-dogs, sodas and milkshakes, soft ice cream, chocolate bars, Walt Disney's lovable world full of cute characters, comic books, Hollywood movies—drew us away from the more conservative and serious traditions at home and at school. Our view of America was conditioned by the kinds of things we associated it with, most of which were frivolous and wonderful.

Plastic came in the form of Reliable toys. Other synthetics such as Bakelite, Lucite and Vinylite followed. Nylon arrived in the shape of transparent nylon blouses which teachers and moms wore under the jackets of their suits. They washed amazingly, and were new, so you got one. Cars began to burst out of their conservatism; they came in funny bulbous shapes, sprouted fins, fishtails and Mae West bumpers and had tinted windows and a wider variety of colours. Automatic transmission arrived, as did hardtop convertibles with no division between the side windows; you could roll all the windows down and bask in the breeze. These new products made life easier and easier. The world of leisure, frivolity and illusion they offered threatened the serious values of hard work, home and family, school and church, which had been supported and given form by Britain.

The parents, good, solid, church-going people, with ingrained traditional values, continued to devote their energy to building a home and raising children. They began to make more money than they had expected to, but, having been through two wars and a depression, they'd learned to make hay while the sun shone and weren't about to let up. The standard of living was already comfortable, with home, marriage, children, cleanliness, health, love, charity work and the church providing the basics. If some people happened to make money too, they were just lucky.

In Riverview, a fairly unpretentious and dignified area, changes were not manifested by any sort of ostentatious display, but prosperity showed in small ways. Homes began to be remodelled. There is a difference between remodelling a home and renovating it. Renovation, as practised in the seventies, respectfully scrapes away the cumulative layers of paint and dirt to restore a house to its original condition. But since the parents of the fifties had grown up in oppressive Victorian houses with dark colours and heavy woodwork, what they wanted to do was cover up the ugly old stuff, and that's what remodelling meant. So the wooden exteriors of houses were stuccoed over and painted. Fieldstone, a material with suggestions of California warmth, began to show up around the steps of houses and around gardens—Ellett's restaurant, Sophie's Hair Styling, the Carson and McCracken houses. Old coal furnaces with their clinkers and coal chutes were converted to oil. Inspired by the interiors shown in *Better Homes and Gardens*, *Ladies' Home Journal* and *Good Housekeeping*, people began to be interested in interior decorating. Porcelain sinks were replaced by stainless steel ones, some with magical 'garburetors'. Using the new plywood and their new power tools, fathers built in kitchen cupboards and counters and covered the counters with arborite. Asphalt and rubber tile laid in the best do-it-yourself tradition replaced linoleum. Chrome and arborite kitchen tables and chairs replaced the old wooden ones. Walls between living rooms and dining rooms were knocked out; the floors were blessed with expensive new wall-to-wall broadloom. Wall-to-wall drapes that pulled together under a valance board replaced the old flowered ones that hung at the sides of the windows. Radiators were covered up, woodwork painted over and walls done in pastel colours. Blond furniture replaced the dark traditional pieces. The word of the day was 'built-in', and the more things you could build in, the better.

The test of a father's do-it-yourself skill was the rec room, an extra room reclaimed from the basement that could act as a safety valve for the bursting energy of growing teenagers. To be a real rec room, it had to have been built by the father. He stapled the new acoustic tile to the ceiling and covered the walls with the new wood that could be put up in panels—striated wood or plywood with a raised grain which had been painted gold and then another colour over top, then rubbed so the gold showed through with the grain. He tiled the floor and down there went the old overstuffed wartime chesterfield, the trilights, the stand-up ashtrays and perhaps an electric fireplace with flickering artificial coals. Picture windows with plate glass replaced the old ones with panes, and doors were fitted with ripply glass; egg crate dividers showed up in kitchens. The old dark United Church style was concealed by pastel woodwork and built-in cupboards.

Plastic portable radios that worked with flashlight batteries arrived. Power mowers replaced the old mechanical ones that were so hard to push, and people had their first experiences of being wakened up on Sunday morning by the put-put of a neighbour cutting his grass. Radio combinations, with a three-speed record player and a radio in an attractive cabinet were also new and everyone got one. And what was a rec room without a ping pong table?

But having acquired most of the things needed for the home, people sensed there was a line to be drawn at freezers, dishwashers and perhaps television. Other things had been necessary, but from here on things were superfluous. The values of people who were ministers or teachers, civil servants or lawyers, did not change. But those who began to make more money moved beyond necessity to acquisition. Some people, those with spiritual values who believed wholeheartedly in the authority of the Bible, foresaw with dread what the advent of materialism meant.

American technology didn't stop at the necessities; it continued to provide people with more things to buy, which they did to keep up with other people who were buying them. A bigger and better car every year, if you could manage it. A mink stole. A home movie camera. A summer cottage with a motor boat.

People acquired these things not because they wanted to solve the problems presented by their old car, or own a beautiful fur, or really go back to nature, but to maintain and increase their stature in their own eyes as well as in the eyes of their neighbours. Superfluous possessions had a bad effect; young boys found their eyes stealing over to the neighbours' yard to compare their car to their own fathers'. The guy with the bigger car was better. People were intimidated by men with big cars and big boats who laughed 'har har har' like Americans, and yet they tried to be like them. Real human values began to be given less weight than material values. Things became more important than people. People were judged by their possessions. Material possessions made the weak equal to the strong, the stupid equal to the smart; they were democratic. Materialism was anti-intellectual and anti-authoritarian.

Many of the same people who were bound to church tradition, active in the community and faithful marriage partners, who didn't drink, didn't flirt, went to church, played bridge, were good neighbours, they too did a lot of the acquiring. They were committed to permanent situations, and the terms of their lives had been set long ago. Growth was not seen in personal, intellectual or spiritual terms; it was seen in material terms. Moving upwards meant owning more things.

The people at first looked up with innocence to the fine objects they could now possess, and felt a bit unworthy. It was a long time before people were at ease with them. It took a woman a long time to be comfortable wearing a mink stole in public; aware that she could be accused of flaunting it in front of women in muskrat, she felt guilty. People at first thought they couldn't live up to the objects; they had bought them to imitate the movie-star American way of life to which they were aspiring, and were only pretending. Thus, at first, instead of the people controlling the objects, the objects controlled the people.

If someone bought a good camera, for example, it wasn't

because he'd said to himself, I'm interested in photography, I want to learn to take fine pictures and to do that, I'll need a good camera. He might never learn to use the camera at all; he might never even use it. Or he might use it to take the new colour slides while making a trip to Europe, which was the new thing to do. The camera was sort of a cult object that gave the person who owned it power. Developing interests and using the objects skilfully, which might have alleviated some of the guilt of owning them and would have made it possible to enjoy them, seemed almost to spoil the possession.

The control and possession of objects transferred itself to the control and possession of children. Authority got mixed up with power. Parents pushed the child to do things they wanted him to do, and stopped him from doing things he wanted to do. Instead of praising or accepting a child when he did something independent, they criticized him; the parents didn't want him to be independent because they might lose control of him. The effect of telling a child to do everything was to rob him of initiative; so he began to think that anything he did on his own was bad, or that he was incapable of doing anything successfully on his own. If he always did as he was told, he was controlled by his parents. If he disobeyed their authority, he was rebelling, would get into trouble and would be punished. It was a double bind.

There was no real understanding of people or of the dynamics of power in relationships, no awareness of why people had quirks or what caused them, no admission of the undercurrents in human relations. People trusted authority, not their feelings. People didn't really know they were controlled by material objects and by an authority corrupted by political forces they weren't aware of. People didn't run the risk of being considered a kook or a square or a communist, by taking a chance with odd behaviour. Nobody rocked the boat. People were really afraid of communists, not because they understood communism, or capitalism, but because they were being programmed to be afraid. Communists stood for the dark forces of anarchy, disorder, degeneracy, lack of structure, and were thought to be infiltrating everywhere. There was no real political awareness whatsoever.

The people who acquired material possessions still went to church on Sunday. There was no contradiction, they simply did both at once. After all, businessmen rationalized, the church was a business too. The result was the *Reader's Digest* mentality, a combination of a sincere belief in God and the Bible, stifled by comfort and security. The children, however, wondered how one could worship Christ in a mink stole. God the Father went hand in hand with keeping up with the Joneses. But traditional values were simply too narrow to cope with the flood of new possibilities opened up by American technology.

There was just too much of a good thing. There was the sunshine, grass and good clean air of Riverview. The security of prairie uneventfulness. The security of marriage, of a warm house in winter with snug padded rooms. The security of health, of youth, of good people to help you, of father's job and mother's love and good meals. The security of public morality forbidding mention of sex, violence or bad language. Life was stuffed with security. It filled the air around you like cotton batting. You had no idea of what it felt like to need something. You knew only good; you had no idea of what bad was at all.

Television

That any sort of outside cultural influence penetrated Winnipeg's
geographic isolation and insulation was something of a miracle.
From the States, we had magazines—the *Saturday Evening Post*
(a major institution with Norman Rockwell and various serial
stories), the *Ladies' Home Journal, McCall's, Good Housekeeping, Redbook, Family Circle, Better Homes and Gardens.* (As
well, there were Canadian publications: *Maclean's, Saturday
Night* and the *Financial Post.*) There were the comic books, the
movies at the Park, the radio programmes and of course the hit
parade, with Patti Page, Teresa Brewer, Rosemary Clooney, the
Ames Brothers, the Mills Brothers, the Andrew Sisters, Les Paul
and Mary Ford, Johnny Ray and Fats Domino. But it was only
when television arrived in Winnipeg in 1954 that we finally got the
full blast of American culture.

Previously, we kids might only have seen television in motels
on car trips in the States. Television was regarded as an amazing
invention, the ultimate technological miracle. A picture show,
right in your own home! However, at the same time, it was viewed
with some apprehension. Picture shows were only for Friday or
Saturday nights. Wasn't it immoral to have access to entertainment all the time? Of course, once the neighbours gave in,
people had to get a set too. Lionel Moore's father appeared on
Country Calendar, a Winnipeg Sunday afternoon programme,
and the Moores were the first in their district to get a set; their
house was always full of kids. Once the set was in the house, and
its novelty wore off, it was bound to change things considerably,
and not for the better. People who previously had other things to
do saw themselves being sucked into watching silly programmes.
TV required no effort, it was like a drug. People chastised themselves for spending so much time watching, and felt guilty about
it, yet found it hard to resist. Bridge parties were dissolved early by

people wanting to watch TV. Instead of talking to each other, which took effort, they'd sit saying nothing until it was time to go home. Television caused arguments over what programme to watch and made large noisy inroads into peaceful homes.

People accorded the invention itself respect, but the content of its programmes did not live up to the invention's ingenuity. Some of the first American programmes that Winnipeg saw on TV were: *Howdy Doody* (Howdy was a young cowboy puppet with forty-eight freckles, one for each state); *Lassie*; the *Jackie Gleason Show*, starring Gleason, Audrey Meadows, Art Carney and the June Taylor dancers; Davy Crockett ('Born on a mountain top in Tennessee/Greenest state in the land of the free'); *I Love Lucy*, starring Lucille Ball and Desi Arnaz; the *Ed Sullivan Show*; *Father Knows Best*, with Robert Young; *Our Miss Brooks*, with Eve Arden as a dry Miss Brooks; *December Bride*, with Spring Byington as a mother-in-law; *Perry Como*; *Kookla, Fran and Ollie*; *Groucho Marx*; *Your Show of Shows*, starring Sid Caesar and Imogene Coca; *Dragnet* ('This is the city. Los Angeles. I work here. I'm a cop.' The *Dragnet* theme quickly became an in joke).

Before television, American culture had been tantalizing and magical; we couldn't get enough of it. After television, we were overexposed to it, and it lost a lot of its appeal. The TV shows were contrived to be wholesome, but the result was bland and boring. Except for Elvis Presley on the *Ed Sullivan Show*, there was nothing to jar the sleepy status quo.

Churchill High School

In 1953, Mr. Scurfield, principal of Lord Roberts School, was asked to head a committee of teachers who wished to have some kind of voice in the planning of a new high school for south Winnipeg, the first new academic high school to be built in the city since 1923. Mr. Scurfield read all the education journals and found four schools that he wanted to visit in Milwaukee, West St. Paul, Minneapolis and Chicago. When he went there, he discovered they'd been painted in rosy hues, so he had to do some more travelling to find other schools. In 1953–54 he and the committee of teachers put together a prospectus on the school proposal, with black and white photographs of the ideal science lab, and so forth. When most classrooms were twenty-eight feet long, Mr. Scurfield was specifying thirty-two-foot classrooms. The science labs were to be thirty-six feet long. Classrooms were to hold thirty movable desks. The head of the school system's building department considered the enlarged classrooms an extravagance, since they would each cost $200 more. Mr. Scurfield defended his specifications with references to the schools he'd visited in the States.

Eventually the new school was built at a cost of a million dollars, a great long building that started at the corner of Arnold and Hay, and stretched along Arnold to the dyke. 'It was one of the best designed schools of all the big new ones', said Mr. Scurfield.

The school struck an ingenious balance between economy and glamour. The architects employed all the latest low-cost functional materials, and incorporated all sorts of new extras. Its twenty-four enlarged classrooms, representing a victory for Mr. Scurfield, stretched lengthwise, six on each side of two floors, along an extended corridor joined by a small entrance hall to an enormous, box-like, official basketball-court-sized gymnasium with a stage at one end. The ceiling was the new acoustic tile, the floor asphalt tile. Cinderblock, used because of its durable surface, lined the corridors between sets of full-length grey metal lockers closed with combination locks. Above the lockers and in the classrooms blond varnished plywood, called 'finished fir', was used.

Every classroom had one continuous wall of windows, the upper two thirds of glass brick, and the lower third a 'vision strip' of clear glass that opened. The wood in the classrooms was all blond, and the blackboards were easy-on-the-eye green. The desks were movable 'single-piece arborite desks', made of green metal-flake tubing holding a blond wood seat and a desk top with an arborite surface.

The gymnasium was an impressive space. Its walls were plaster painted pale green. Its floor was of new compressed wood blocks instead of the slur maple flooring common to most gyms. There were no windows; instead, covered neon lights set into the acoustic tile ceiling were supplemented by twenty-four five-foot-square plexiglass skylights which provided a beautiful natural light. The gym could be divided in half by a great folding plastic-canvas partition, also in pale green. The gym also had athletic equipment rooms, a dressing room off the stage, showers for boys and girls, and a modern kitchen for teas.

There were an unheard-of number of facilities—a cooking laboratory, sewing rooms with built-in electric sewing machines, arts and crafts rooms, music rooms, and four science labs, which appeared to offer students all sorts of new opportunities to learn. The entire inspiration for the school had been drawn from Mr. Scurfield's prospectus, based on the American schools he had visited. And now, here in Riverview, was a first-class American school, the equal of any they had down there.

Mr. Scurfield became principal of the new school. He had two names in mind—Red River School, because the school was right by the Red River, or Churchill School, because the dyke was called Churchill Drive. It was also suggested the school be called Andrew Mynarski High School after a Ukrainian pilot from the north end who was killed in 1946 and received the Victoria Cross. But the name was considered a north-end name, out of place in a south-end school. The name Churchill was chosen, and Mr. Scurfield sent Winston Churchill a letter telling him about the new school bearing his name. Churchill sent back a picture and a signed letter, dated 30 November 1955, which read: 'Thank you so much for your letter. I am indeed honoured that your new school should bear my name, and I am happy to send my good wishes to all the children who will receive their education there'.

Churchill High School is the ultimate Canadian irony—an American-inspired school incorporating all the glamorous extras, having a British façade by being called after a British statesman; the British identity served to conceal from people's consciousnesses the fact that the school was in reality American.

The teachers came from schools all across the city. A goodly number of them Mr. Scurfield brought with him from Lord Roberts. Amongst them were Flossie and Mary Neithercut, two spinster sisters who lived in a beautiful brick house on the corner of Baltimore and Hay. They both had taught at Lord Roberts, both had short, curled grey hair and both wore glasses, suits with straight skirts and blouses under the jackets, Oxfords and, in winter, black seal coats. The vice-principal was Mr. W.J. Madder ('Zorro'), a good-looking, efficient man who did a lot of running around.

The only two teachers from Riverview were Peter Kallos, a tremendously warm and popular teacher, and Charlie Martin, who assumed the mantle of Churchill's guidance teacher. Charlie Martin's previous experience had been as grade seven teacher at Riverview, and his guidance training was slight. But guidance was new and American, having begun in the thirties in the States, and in the Winnipeg of 1955 was just beginning to be taken seriously. There were guidance programmes in several Winnipeg schools and at Riverview Charlie Martin had given home room training, having taken a course in guidance counselling, which included mental and achievement testing. The job of guidance teacher was to help the students choose courses from the variety provided, or to help them with their study habits. It was official and hard-line; it had nothing to do with students' personal problems. Guidance at the time was considered a soft American touch; one wasn't supposed to need that sort of help, and the guidance counsellor was a little suspicious, as he seemed to be doing what parents were supposed to do, and his presence suggested parents weren't doing their job. But Charlie Martin took on the glamour job and did his best.

In 1955, students in Winnipeg high schools were divided at grade ten into two streams—matriculation or commercial. Matriculation was the course which included two languages and two sciences through grades ten and eleven, and led into university. Commercial led only to a high school certificate, and was mostly for girls who intended to be secretaries. Graduating from grade eleven was 'getting your junior matric'. Senior matric was grade twelve, which was the equivalent of first-year university. From grade eleven, you could go out into first year at the University of Manitoba campus in Fort Garry or to United College downtown. Or you could remain in school for grade twelve, and get your senior matric and go into second year after that.

The home rooms, of course, were divided up according to which stream kids were in and which combination of options they had. There was a suspicion too that rooms were divided up according to marks: all the bright kids in one room, and so on down the line. But it appears that keeping groups of friends intact was a big consideration.

We awaited the first day of school at Churchill with more than the usual dread, for it meant the end of the Golden Age of Riverview. We would be lumped in with all kinds of Lord Roberts kids whom we didn't know, and taught by alien, enemy Lord Roberts teachers. And not only that, but the very principal of Churchill was the former Lord Roberts principal, the dreaded Mr. Scurfield, scourge of Riverview.

There must have been an angel in the wings, because Room 8, Miss East's room, kept our group of friends intact. It was the double option room; the kids took Latin to be with their friends anyway. There we all were, all the Riverview goody-goodies plus some of the most popular and attractive Lord Roberts bad boys. There were Fran, Sue, Melinda and Barb. John Hodges had been going to take typing, but switched at the last minute to take Latin, and was in Room 8, along with John Malo, Lionel Moore, Cliff Leach and the two star athletes from Lord Roberts, John Kemp and Alan Ackland. As if that wasn't enough, the girls who were taking home ec were moved to another room, a switch which left nine girls with twenty-nine boys. We couldn't believe our luck.

Dress

The teenager, complete with slang and casualness, could be nothing but an American concept. To be a real teenager, you had to drink Cokes, eat hamburgers (known as nips in Winnipeg, because the local Salisbury House chain, started by R.M. Erwin, an American, in the thirties, sold them as such), French fries (known in Winnipeg as chips, in the English tradition), go to the Dairy Queen, listen to the Top Forty and neck. The realities of Winnipeg, the weather and the geographic isolation, plus the relative scarcity of money, limited the degree to which American culture could be assimilated. Most boys could not afford cars, so did their cruising on racing bikes, and the Canadian teenager's style lacked the voluptuousness of that of the American. But where there were no styles available to copy, teenage ingenuity invented them.

The boys and girls in grades ten and eleven at Churchill were between the ages of fifteen and eighteen. The boys were just beginning to be attractive, and to experience the first rush of masculine power. They were tall, some of them, and starting to fill out; their voices had deepened and already some of them had that masculine presence that makes girls' toes tingle. The girls were beginning to have curves and breasts, were starting to wear brassieres, girdles, nylons, lipstick, and both sexes had begun the ritual of primping in the washroom. Physical attractiveness was assuming importance all round.

There were two areas of achievement for boys, school work and sports. Whereas the parental attitudes of the society and the school system emphasized marks, sports were far more important to kids because it was in that arena that a boy proved to his friends that he was a man. A boy who wasn't particularly good in school could compensate by excelling on the football field, hockey rink, basketball court or baseball diamond. Although sports provided an alternative system of goals and values and fostered teamwork and brotherhood, they weren't any more democratic than school-work, because outstanding athletic abilities were as rare as out-standing brains. But they were the field where boys could display their grace and litheness, and decorate the basic skills with their own flair and style, especially in front of girls. So basically there were two types of boys—the brains and the athletes.

The usual dress for ordinary guys and for brains was a plain or plaid shirt over a T-shirt, and sometimes a V-neck or Perry Como sweater, grey or charcoal grey with red and white stripes down to the three buttons at the bottom, cords or chinos and or-dinary shoes.

The athletes, however, had a style all their own. They were The Men, the rocks or hardrocks. To them, girls were just a passing attraction. Sports were everything. Churchill High School opened without a football team. Football was expensive, and the support of the business community had to be recruited, and wasn't top priority for a new academic high school. The many good football players in the South End who attended Churchill were pretty miffed. Since they still wanted to play football, they had to go to the west end, out Arlington, and play for teams like the West End Memorials or the West End Rams. Being interested enough in football to go way out there while still going to school meant that guys were fairly independent of the school and of their parents; the guys rejected the implication that football wasn't im-portant, and went on playing. Playing on a team outside the school improved a guy's status, and carried a lot of weight with the girls. From these outside teams, guys got 'ball jackets' in the team colours— a Lions jacket was a black Melton cloth windbreaker that fastened with snaps, with white leather sleeves, ribbed wrists and waists and lots of pile in the Lions emblem on the chest and in the lettering across the front. These jackets were a mark of status, indicating that the wearer was 'one of the boys'. Churchill later issued red, white and blue basketball jackets, but these didn't pack the punch of the originals.

The Men were an elite that existed independent of the school. They scorned the school. They sat at the back of the room and goofed off. Schoolwork was sissy stuff. Guys who studied hard and tried to get good marks were 'suckholes', sucking up to the teachers for approval. Guys who were both good in school and in sports, like John Hodges and Cliff Leach, had the respect of both suckholes and athletes, but guys who were kind of mommas' boys and squares were scoffed at.

The Men wore their jackets indoors and out, in class, to parties, bowling, to the show, everywhere, day in and day out. They also wore drapes, a fashion peculiar to Winnipeg, invented and made by the local garment industry for its benefit. The style began about 1950 and ended about 1957. Drapes were like zoot suit pants, wide at the knee and tight at the ankle. The more extreme the ratio of knee width to ankle width, the better the drapes. When the knee was really wide and the ankle really tight, the pants were called balloon drapes. You usually ordered them tailor-made at Eaton's, although there was also a ready-made black denim type with white snaps that was popular. They were expensive too, and came in a wide variety of checks and colours. You could have one, two or three seams down the side. They were high-waisted, and the belt slipped through wide loops on which you could have one, two or three buttons. The pockets at the back also had flaps that buttoned down with one, two or three buttons; usually if you had three seams, you'd have three buttons everywhere. Some of the back flaps were shaped like gun holsters; these were called gun-flap pockets. The girls all had drapes too. They were flattering, in a funny way. In the summer, the boys would wear light unbelted denim pants that were elasticized at the back; this style initiated a fad of pulling people's pants down.

With their drapes, the boys would wear evil pointy black shoes. In winter, they wore rubber galoshes that closed with buckles. It was *de rigueur* to do up only the first two or three buckles nearest the toe, and leave the rest flapping open, so the guys would clink like cowboys in spurs or knights in armour as they walked along.

Boys were very conscious of their hair and combed it a lot. The athletes among the boys, like Kemp and Ack, usually wore brushcuts because they didn't get in the way. The boys who had longer hair used Brylcreem, which was advertised on sports telecasts. Some of the more progressive boys wore what was called a Bogie or a Boogie cut; this consisted of a brushcut on top, with the sides long and meeting in the back in a ducktail. Bogie cuts had a way of falling forward around the guy's ears, and required a lot of attention to keep that from happening. John Hodges had a Bogie cut, and spent a lot of time on it; characteristically, his ducktail always met perfectly at the back. He also polished the sleeves of his ball jacket with white shoe-polish.

The girls still had to wear tunics and white blouses to school three days a week. There was a regulation length for tunics, usually six or nine inches above the knee, which looked awful. Every so often, the phys. ed. teacher would crack down and come around with a yardstick, and make girls kneel down so she could measure how high the tunic was above the knee.

But nobody wore their tunic six inches above the knee any more; nobody wore the regulation two-button belt that came with it: sure signs that parental authority was being overthrown. Instead of the belt, you wore a special black knitted tie you could buy at Eaton's and have cut off at the length you wanted. You tied this around your waist in a Windsor knot, so you could slide it up and tighten it. The ends of the tie you frayed so they made a nice fringe. You always wore one end long and one end short. The relationship between the short end and the long end said a lot about the girl. If they were about the same length, she was a good girl. But if one end was pulled very short and the other hung almost to the ground, wow. These ties were called 'tails'.

The tunic converted into a very sexy little outfit. You didn't shorten it, because, officially, it was supposed to be six inches above the knee. Instead, you pulled the tunic up over the tie and bloused it out nicely all round. This way, when the teacher came around with her yardstick, you could take off the belt, and lo and behold, it would be six inches above the knee, and as soon as she was out of sight, you could hike it up to the top of your thigh again. You wore a garter belt, long black stockings and blue pants. Since the tunic was so short, you had to keep pulling up your stockings at the back, as gaps would appear between the stocking and the blue pants every time you sat down, plus you had to keep rearranging the tunic pleats and blousing operation. With the tunic, you still wore the regulation white shirt and tie, but you sort of rolled the sleeves of the shirt half way to the elbow and left the collar open and turned it up, so the points stuck out like Beau Brummel's. To have the collar turned up all the way at the back, and the tips arching out like wings was the height of fashion. Keeping a tunic happening required constant primping and sexy little gestures that got the boys' attention.

When girls were not wearing tunics, they wore girdles or the new Playtex panty girdles and white cotton or satin brassieres, like the Gothic Petalburst. Brassieres were designed to produce points, and you pulled them up as high as possible. A softer look was preferable, but brassieres that produced it were hard to come by. Girdles sealed over the cleft in the buttocks, and made the behind look like a torch singer's, which was a desirable look. Skirts were also based on the torch-singer line; they zipped up the back, were tight to mid-calf and on each side had kick-pleats that flared out like fishtails as you walked. With the skirt, you might wear a Kitten or Grand'mere twin sweater set. You wore them both, with only the bottom three buttons of the cardigan done up, simulating a Perry Como sweater. The orlon sweater had the added attraction of clinging to your breasts. Winnipeg winters are full of static electricity, and when you took your coat off, the sweater would cling and crackle.

Over that, you'd wear a baggy jean jacket that closed with white snaps, much baggier than a Levi windbreaker. Your hair was usually done in a ducktail, which wasn't very attractive on girls, especially at the nape of the neck, where it had a tendency to degenerate into an oily fringe. You'd arrange curls in front, and kiss curls stiffened with soap at the sides. There were also pixie cuts and poodle cuts and bustles that required permanents. And on your head, in the winter, you'd wear a babushka, a Ukrainian peasant fashion, a silk kerchief tied under the chin. Except you'd wear it pulled way back from your forehead to show your kiss curls, which were often held in place by hair clips, as if they were getting ready for something big. 'Canoe' shoes, oily brown leather moccasins, were very in; you also might wear boys' black and white runners with ankle socks, saddle shoes, and later white bucks. All shoes were worn with nylons with seams in them and white ankle socks, usually rolled down. With all that (and of course your white lipstick under the Kissing or Shocking Pink), you were ready to take on Mario Lanza.

Everybody used three-ring binders with leatherette covers that zipped on three sides. The big manly ones had two-inch rings and the punier ones had rings of one and a half inches. Inside you put your Campus looseleaf notebooks, one for each subject, divided by stick-on plastic tabs on which you printed the name of the subject. You filled in the timetable on the front, and wrote your name in the space provided. You put your pens and pencils in the middle of the rings. The school gave out paper book covers with which you covered your textbooks. You put two books side by side inside the binder, and any other junk that would fit, and zipped the whole works up. The rest of the books you'd put side by side on top; you had to take them home with you after four to do your homework, and bring them back to school with you the next day. Soon the looseleaf notebooks would be covered with blotchy doodles from primitive Paper Mates, the covers on your books would get fuzzy and tear and the zipper on your binder would rip from your trying to put too much stuff inside. Some binders developed fantastic character in one term. The guys would clink along with their binder held on their hip with one hand. But the girls carried theirs in front, under their breasts. Holding your books tight against your chest pushed your breasts up even more.

Boys would often carry your books for you, or throw them in the snow. Now it was different walking to and from school. Instead of splashing through puddles and walking along the tops of snow ridges, and making snow angels, kids turning into people walked slowly, and when it came time to part on a street corner, they dragged the parting out, standing there talking, stubbing toes in the snow.

From behind our books and under our babushkas, we regarded school with mild amusement, an unfortunate intrusion into our social lives. School wasn't what life was about, but it made all these demands on our time. Still, it had to be gone to, and with a sigh, we went.

High School

One of the basic problems with school, 'period' (an expression of the times) was its regimentation. We had to line up outside the door to get in; we had to line up outside the classroom to get in; we had to get up when the bell went at the end of a class and line up outside another classroom. Days were punctuated by bells. Having to move around all the time made us feel dispossessed.

The lecture method of teaching, with the teacher standing at the front of the room and the class subserviently listening, didn't help. The teacher had control of the class; to ask a question, the student raised his hand, and hoped the teacher would pick up on it. There was no encouragement of discussion. Kids were forbidden to talk to one another in class. You were supposed to sit there passively and have your little mind moulded.

The teacher took the textbook and went through it in the year. The teacher would set a page of problems for the day, or a chapter to read. You would take them home, do the problems, read the chapter and come back the next day, when the teacher would go over the problems with the class, have members of the class read parts of the chapter, explain it a bit and then set another chapter and more problems. You weren't supposed to read beyond a specified page, or even so much as peek at the next page of problems, and so you didn't. The teacher took the responsibility for getting you through the book. If you did it yourself, you'd spoil it for yourself, because you'd only have to go through it all again at the pace of the whole class. It wasn't much of a challenge. You'd sit there listening to each tick of the minute hand on the big black and white clock overhead, as it inched towards the end of the period.

The tedium and regimentation encouraged a lot of game-playing among the kids. Lineups were times for boys to pull girls' tails, or muss each other's ducktails, or press on kids' books so they'd all fall to the floor, or pull down their pants.

Mr. Norris Belton taught social studies. A man with a grey brushcut, who wore glasses that magnified his eyes, rumpled blue blazers and grey flannels, his teaching style was to have the class underline important phrases in the social studies textbook. His classes consisted of forty minutes of his reading a few pages, and stopping every few words so kids could underline an important phrase. What happened of course was that you became an expert underliner. You'd underline some phrases with single lines and some with double lines, and quickly got the knack of whipping out your ruler and drawing perfect lines. What the lines were under didn't sink in very far.

In physics, we had science notebooks which had a blank page on the left side and lined pages on the right. On the blank page, we drew a picture of the test tubes, alcohol burners, iron stands, clamps and beakers and on the right we wrote up the experiment under the headings of Object, Apparatus, Method, Observations and Conclusions. Since understanding the experiment was not that difficult, the object became to produce a meticulous notebook, with eye-catching drawings—little marks around flames to show they were glowing, fingers holding matches, candles that looked as if they'd been copied from Christmas cards, little wagons rolling down inclined planes with cartoon marks around the wheels to show they were turning and shading under the inclined plane, tuning forks standing like Dali trees casting long thin shadows, each emitting musical notes with ripply stems like Tweety Bird's. John Hodges' first consciousness of Marianne Patchell, later his wife, dated from the time Mr. Bell held up her science notebook as an example for all to follow.

Standing at the front of the class, teachers were at the mercy of student scrutiny, and the kids got their revenge. Mr. Scurfield was no exception. Known as Scuff, he wore his hair combed straight back from his forehead in a pompadour; he had bristly eyebrows and a large nose, and his mouth had a way of dropping open emptily for a moment before he said something. He also had a tendency to pontificate. He would stand up at the front of a classroom he'd dropped into for a few moments, in his brown suit, with his glasses in one hand and a paper in the other. He would put his glasses on to read something from the paper, then snatch them off to address the class, as if speaking to a very large audience, elbow tucked to his side, chest out. He'd whip the glasses back on again to look at the paper, then whip them off again.

One French teacher, Miss Loutit, had long black hair

streaked with grey, which she braided and put up on top of her head or let hang down her back in a plait; she was kind of artistic. She wore glasses with pink plastic rims, no makeup, black sweaters with a hanky tucked in at the wrist and the sweater tucked into a pleated skirt. She slouched with her hips forward and her spine curved over. The boys were fascinated by her breasts, which looked as if two handkerchiefs had been stuffed into her sweater. She was a dreamy soul, often carried away, and likely she soared above reality so high that she never heard herself referred to as Miss Lowtits.

Since all the school equipment was brand new, the teachers in charge of it were inclined to be a bit possessive. Mary Neithercut, who had charge of the brand new library, wouldn't let you take a book out. You could read it there, though. For a while. Reevan Cramer, the art teacher, however, gave kids full use of all kinds of great stuff—chisels for wood and stone cutting, poster paints, letraset, India Ink, his kiln for copper enamelling, lino cutting tools, everything. His room was constantly a beehive of creative activity.

School was memorizing, homework, this rational thing you did with your mind. What could an inclined plane or sine and cosine possibly have to do with the life we were living? No attempt was made to bridge the gap; schoolwork existed in its own vacuum, and was shunted to one side by who was going with whom and got in the way of extracurricular activities. Competition for marks was private and personal, and since the work wasn't hard it gave way to competition to be in activities.

At the beginning of the year, student elections were held. Each class elected a president and a vice-president, usually the most popular kid in the room. The president and vice-president got to be on the student council. The election for student council president was more formal, with a campaign, posters, nominations and speeches in the gymnasiums. The candidates the first year were Gordy Webster, Murray Brueckner and Janet Cameron. Gordy won. Janet was a girl so she got to be vice-president, and Murray got to be secretary-treasurer, so nobody really lost. The student council dealt with such portentous issues as who were going to be the convenors of the school tea.

There were piles of committees to be on—the constitution committee, the publicity and art committee, the frolic committee, and the yearbook committee, which had lots of committees of its own. There was the debating club, the school orchestra, the choirs. There were sports—soccer, speed skating, curling, basketball, volleyball, hockey, a tumbling club, and a boys' sports council.

There was track and field. For participation in these you got points toward a school letter.

There was a tendency to be in as many things as you could. Who at fifteen knew how to be selective? Moreover, we didn't want to feel left out, and so were encountering our own keep up with the Joneses syndrome. John Hodges, for example, was class president, on the student council, a member of the publicity and art committee, assistant editor of the yearbook and a member of the art layout and photography committee for the yearbook; he played senior high soccer, curled, speed skated, tumbled and was on the sports council; and his wooden sculpture, an African-inspired figure covering its crotch with its hands, which he named 'Adam after the Fall', was published in the yearbook.

One job that had to be done was to establish the school's identity through colours, symbols, logos and words. Once the identification with Sir Winston Churchill was made, the rest was easy. School colours? Maroon, white and royal blue, of course, like the Union Jack. Basketball uniforms, school jackets and soccer sweaters were designed accordingly. Motto? Victory, what else? That's what the yearbook was called, *The Victory*. John Hodges designed the cover symbol, a big V, with two stylized torches as its arms, which contained the letters CHS, in red, white and blue. He also designed the school logo, a V with a torch in the centre, and the letters CHS on a banner underneath, to be used on school rings, identification bracelets, tie clips, cufflinks and pins. The first year's *Victory* was planned on the structure of the British government, with the principal as Prime Minister, the vice-principal as the Chancellor of the Exchequer, and so on down through the Guard of Honour, the House of Lords, the House of Commons, the Privy Council, Hansard and Ministry of Health and Welfare.

The school mascot? A bulldog, with its associations of tenaciousness and grit. A live English bulldog called Winston was accordingly obtained and made an appearance at all basketball games, where, in his little blue coat, he'd bark at the running shoes pounding by his nose down the compressed wood floor. With a live mascot, Churchill was truly an American high school.

At basketball games, which, because Churchill didn't have a football team, became fairly important, cheerleaders wore blue satin pleated skirts and white turtle-neck sweaters, waved red and white paper pompoms and cheered.

We've got the t-e-a-m
That's on the b-e-a-m

> We've got the team
> That's on the beam
> That's really hep to the jive!
> So come on Churchill,
> Skin 'em alive!

At first the school spirit, all the red, white and blue paraphernalia, was a little forced. It took organization, which kids rebelled against, being much more interested in other things, like making wisecracks. So there were constant complaints from the organizing elite about the general apathy and lack of school spirit.

There was a Remembrance Day Service, a Christmas concert and an annual school tea, for which the kids, in the traditional manner, were given tickets to sell from door to door in their neighbourhoods. The Churchill school tea was the only event which brought the community into the school, and, as at Riverview School, it was always a big occasion.

The tea was a most gracious affair. One and all put on their best manners. It was held in the gymnasium where two long tables were set in a cross, covered by a white tablecloth and adorned with a huge arrangement of flowers set in the middle. The beautiful natural lighting from the plexiglass domes above illuminated the white surface of the tablecloth and enriched the colours of the flowers. The gym was ringed with metal chairs. At each of the four ends of the table sat a 'lady' in hat and gloves before a silver tea service lent by one of the district moms, pouring cups of tea and coffee. To be asked to pour tea was an honour; the pourers changed every hour or so. On the table were sterling silver trays lent by district moms; on the trays were paper doilies and on the doilies elegant sandwiches: cream or pimento cheese, egg salad or pickle and meat paste spread on three slices of bread, two brown and one white, or vice versa, with the crusts removed, and cut into finger-sized strips. On other trays were arranged various dainties—little cookies with depressions in them to hold mom's best crab apple jelly, or luscious dream cake, brownies, iced bonbons or matrimonial cake, all home-baked by proud South Fort Rouge moms. A tea was the event in which wifely expertise and delicacy came to the fore; without moms who worked in charities and used Victorian traditions to raise money, teas wouldn't have existed.

The atmosphere was hushed, as the parents, sitting around the gym on the metal chairs, chatted with neighbours and teachers, their voices blending in the sound of a dignified, respectful crowd. Girl students were enlisted to serve the tea, sandwiches and dainties. We had to be spotless, our white shirts clean, tunic pleats pressed knife-sharp, hems at a reasonable length, stockings without runs and hair shining. We took our places for the required hour between the arms of the cross, watching the trays or serving. When unsightly spaces began to appear between the sandwiches we'd take them back to the kitchen and get them filled up again by the moms slaving back there. The servers were higher in the hierarchy, since they had contact with the guests. They would go up and ask which it would be and how, and take the order to the pourer, who would pour the cup and add sugar lumps on the saucer with sugar tongs, individual cup by individual cup. When a coffeepot got empty, the pourer, with impeccable manners, would take it in her white-gloved hands and hold polite consultation with the girl nearby, who would practically curtsy as she took the coffeepot ever so gently from the gloved hands and tiptoed ever so gently across the floor under the eyes of the watching parents to the kitchen. It was like being a maid. Likely the tradition had its origins in colonial attempts to imitate the manners and customs of the Royal Family and British aristocracy. As it was, teas had evolved locally to a high degree of refinement and were rather pleasant.

But to the students who were charged with the honour of waiting on the guests, a school tea brought out that elitist smugness, that 'best behaviour' thing that put us in favour with the teachers. We fell for the prestige which being in with the teachers and parents gave us, which was in fact cultivated in us by them. We were indeed the goody-goodies and suckholes the rejects said we were, betraying our bond with them for the more rewarding bond with those above.

Yet, at the time, there was nothing else for it. Life was straight, hard, absolute. There were the parents, chugging away in the centre of life, doing their best to make good lives for themselves and competing mildly to see who could put the most good things together. There was no bending over to help the disadvantaged, except in traditional charity work. The poor were relegated to their level and stayed there. And so it was that the kids didn't bend, because it was wrong to. We were encouraged to extend ourselves as far as we could academically. And those who fell short, fell short, period.

Social Life

School kept kids pretty busy, with practices, teas, games and schoolwork, but the most important thing was what was happening socially. Social life inside the school extended to social life outside the school. Since everybody lived nearby, went to the same places, was around and available, social contact was going on virtually all the time.

The action swung back and forth among school, the Top and the Community Club. And to get from one to the other, you walked. We walked to and from school with our friends. On Friday nights, we picked up our friends at their houses and walked down to the Teen Canteen, the dance at the Club. After the Canteen, we walked up to Ellett's for a thirteen-inch hot dog. Then three of us would walk the fourth home, and so on. It was usual for boys to walk girls home, a practice which gentlemanly stoicism took to ludicrous lengths. Even if the boy lived a mile in the other direction, he'd walk the girl home, and then walk all the way back himself in forty below weather.

Walking became a moving party. It was nice. We would walk along the snowy road, strung out in a line, the boys making wisecracks, their galoshes clinking and squeaking. A light snowfall might be descending and we would stand on the street with our mouths turned up, trying to catch snowflakes. It was very quiet and very cold, with the black night and the white snow. Breath steamed in the air. Our mouths would go funny and not work right and our noses ran as we tried to hold serious conversations. When we got to a street corner, if one was going one way and the others were going the other, the whole gang would stand under the streetlight, jumping up and down in one spot to keep the circulation going, laughing and talking, not wanting to go home to parents and bed.

Greeves Restaurant, on the west side of Osborne Street, was

the headquarters for the Lord Roberts bad boys, Al Ackland, John Kemp and their tougher friends. The bad boys stood on the corner of Beresford and Osborne in their ball jackets and drapes, checking all the cars. If they were going to the Park, they'd meet at Greeves and go on to the theatre; if they were going to the Canteen, they'd meet at Greeves and go on to the Canteen. And after the show or Canteen, they'd all go back to Greeves.

Kemp was a good example of how the Top figured in a bad boy's relationship to school. Kemp couldn't stand school. He could hardly wait to get out. He used to think up distractions, such as having coffee with the janitors. When Mr. Scurfield caught him and asked him what he thought he was doing, Kemp said, 'I'm having coffee.' The next day, when a teacher sent him out of class to report to Mr. Scurfield, Scuff gave him one look and said, 'I suppose you want donuts now.'

Kemp couldn't study. But one day, he said to himself, 'By Jesus, I'm going to get good marks, and I'm going to study.' He sat down after supper, and spread out his books in front of him, and started in. He had an exam the next morning. No sooner had he sat down than the phone rang. It was his buddy, Duke.

'What are you doing, Kemp?'

'I'm studying. *You* know.'

'You're *what*?'

'I'm studying. I'd like to get good marks.'

'Well, that's too bad.'

'Why?'

'Well, we're all meeting at Greeves and we're gonna go to the show, there's a helluva show on.'

'Yeah?' says Kemp, in a strained voice. Then he says, 'Nope. I'm gonna study.' He hung up the phone, sat down again and was reading and reading, when he thought, 'Aw shit,' and before he knew it, he was down at Greeves, catching up to Duke. And when the marks were read off after the exam, they heard—this girl, ninety-eight; this guy, a hundred; Duke Tait, two; John Kemp six. And Kemp would say, 'There you are, Duke, I studied harder'n you.'

Some Riverview kids would drop into Greeves for sunflower seeds and kibitz with the waitresses after bowling in the Kit Kats league Saturday mornings at the Park Alleys. But most Riverview kids felt too young, and would go to Ellett's after bowling and look over at the older kids going into Greeves.

The bad boys from Lord Roberts had reputations; they were known as 'hard rocks' or 'hoods'. They did things. Like one

Hallowe'en, the bad boys siphoned a tank of gasoline and spread it across Osborne Street near Ellett's. They figured when they lit it, it would only go about knee-high. But it went right up to the trolley bus wires, and cars were backed up on both sides of a solid wall of flame. The bad boys nearly had a bird.

The rocks were the first to start drinking. They would park up at the Liquor Commission and ask somebody who was going in to get them a bottle. Guys who looked older than their age would go in and get it themselves, but Kemp, who was blond and always looked the youngest, had to get somebody to buy his for him. The bad boys matured earlier than the Riverview kids who hung around Ellett's, playing the juke box and listening to their favourite songs in an atmosphere of innocence and safety.

It's probable that if the Park Alleys hadn't been at the Top, none of us would have learned to bowl. But the owner, Mr. Bradshaw, a warm fatherly man who also worked at the racetrack, set up the Kit Kats on Saturday mornings, and hosted a school bowling league as well. Boys like Lionel Moore and John Hodges worked as pinboys for thirty-five cents an hour. It was dangerous work, because the pins would fly around. They'd have to set them up, and leap out of the way. We tried to bowl on an alley where somebody we knew was working, because we might have more luck.

The Park Alleys had a special smell, a combination of smoke, sweat and damp feet in rented bowling shoes. It had two rows of red wooden benches with holes in the back where you put your Coke when your turn came up. There were the sounds of people cheering a strike, the smooth sound of the balls rolling down the shiny alleys, the chink as they hit a pin, or the chink chink chink as the pins tumbled, then silence, the hum of the balls rolling back up, popping up through a cloth and knocking against each other like china bowls as they came to rest. Five-pin or duck-pin bowling was a rewarding game in which you could accumulate a big fat score fairly easily.

But more than bowling went on at the Park Alleys. Bowling was an excuse for cruising and catching a girl's eye. A good bowler, usually, one of the good athletes, in his ball jacket and drapes, stood for a long moment taking aim while the girls watched. He pussyfooted up to the line with his personal flair, let the ball go and stood motionless, or perhaps hopping on one foot. He betrayed no emotion, except to flick his hand through his hair to replace the bogie cut which had fallen over his ears. A muscle might jump in his cheek the way he'd seen Audie Murphy's do in

The Red Badge of Courage at the Park. A heroic muscle twitching in a cheek also reminded the girl of Audie Murphy whom she too had seen at the Park. Girls weren't expected to bowl well. Better they should walk up and dump the ball on the alleys with two hands than compete with the boys. Girls were there mainly to watch the boys, and compare their styles. The boys, the heroes, would check to see who was watching them. It was very intense; a disappointed boy would be lavishly consoled by the girls, for, if he didn't do well, his reputation as one of the boys would suffer.

Fran, Sue, Barb and I, instead of going to the Park alone, began to go there with boys. The hoods and rocks, with their dates wearing babushkas and Shocking Pink lipstick and chewing gum, met regularly at the third aisle-light down, and would be strung out all across one row. Going to the Park became more difficult, now that boys were in the picture, as there were some boys you wanted to avoid who turned up at the Park the same night you did.

Teen Canteen dances were held in a new addition built onto Riverview Community Club in 1955. It had a peaked ceiling, a tile floor and windows looking out onto the playground and the skating rink.

Lionel Moore was president of the Teeners at the Club. He'd grown into a lanky character who wore a green melton cloth hockey jacket from his Club hockey team, cords, the inevitable galoshes and usually a golf hat pulled over his eyes. His mouth was custom-made for wisecracking and gum-chewing, and, though he was only sixteen, his voice was low and bullfroggy.

As Lord of the Canteens, Lionel got somebody to run the record player, asked a couple of parents to supervise, hired an off-duty cop and sat at a table outside the door of the new part, stamping hands, selling tickets from a roll and making wisecracks. The wood-panelled main room, with its floor covered with flattened pieces of cardboard boxes to protect it from skates, with its benches and its snack bar, was full of hockey players. Outside the lights on the hockey rink were still on, and guys might be scraping the rink with wide shovels in toques and Canadiens sweaters, or smacking pucks against the boards. They clambered in off the ice, with their pads and sticks, cheeks cherry-red and stiff, noses running, out of breath. There was the continuous clomp clomp of skates on the floor. The off-duty cop leaned against the door, hat in hand, talking to the parents, keeping an eye out for drunks.

Inside the new part, the lights would be almost out; there was enough light coming in from the lights on the rinks outside and reflecting from their surfaces. The atmosphere was romantic. The boys in their ball jackets would mill around in a stag line by the door, jabbing each other with their elbows, ready to escape. The girls would sit on the metal chairs and wait, in their long straight skirts, canoe shoes, ankle socks and orlon sweaters, with the points thrusting through seductively. They watched from under their Patti Page hairstyles, crossing their ankles to one side as their mothers had shown them. People stuck to the lighted areas by the door and by the record player; the other part was dark and things could get mushy down there.

The girls, the cutest ones, always started the jiving, dancing together to 'Honky Tonk' by Bill Doggett, or 'House of Blue Lights'. They jived in a style that was distinctive to Winnipeg. They held hands, the same hand on each side, and stepped a couple of mincing little steps; on the third beat, they would drop their hands, then join them again. They looked not at one another, but blankly over their partners' shoulders, ultra-cool. The mincing little steps made the buttocks sway, and swished the pleats on the long skirts from side to side. Minimal movement was the living end.

To jive with a boy could be a nerve-wracking experience. When he pushed the girl to swirl, he often pushed her so violently she staggered halfway across the room. Some boys were too short to hold their arms high enough for girls to turn under, which meant the girls would have to scrunch down. Then the boy would cross her arms in front of her, and holding her hands, pull first to one side and then to the other and then pull her arm fast to unwind her, and she'd miss his hand after the spin. Boys seemed to get jiving mixed up with wrestling. All girls wanted to dance with the good dancers, to avoid having their arms wrenched from their sockets. Couples who were going steady usually danced very well, and stayed together all night. The guys with the ball jackets usually danced very well, and had styles all their own. If the boy was tall, he would put his arm straight out on the girl's shoulder, and she'd put her arm on his. He would hold her other hand straight down, and walk along, steering the girl backwards along the floor, looking down at her and talking to her.

As the evening wore on, and he kept dancing with the same girl, her hands would move under his arms or around his neck, and his would move further around her, until they were rocking back and forth in a clinch, ear to ear, shoulder to shoulder and hip to hip. The less sophisticated of us fooled around with the record player or put up with the short, less dangerously sexy partners that stepped on our toes. Afterwards we'd walk up to Ellett's, all except Irene Holt, who lived across Ashland and whose mother wouldn't let her.

Sex

What was it all about? You tell me and we'll both know, as the saying went. Something was happening to us; the moving belt of time was carrying us inexorably away from the innocence of childhood, which our parents could cope with, into dark sinister territory where they didn't want us to go. Still, we had to move on, although they tried to hold us back, and in our very movement forward, they seemed to feel we were doing something wrong. We didn't understand. We didn't understand anything. How could we, never having been there before?

The words to the songs didn't help. None of the songs, not one, was explicit; they intentionally avoided being so, as what they might be explicit about was considered dirty. Most of the songs were for wholesome family listening—'The Shoemaker's Shop', by the Ames Brothers, 'Heart of my Heart', by Dean Martin, 'That's Amore', 'The Bible Tells Me So', 'Round and Round', by Perry Como, 'Young at Heart', by Frank Sinatra. In fact, many of the songs were written for parents. There were high-romantic, semi-classical songs like 'Be My Love', by Mario Lanza, and songs by his runner-up, Frank Ifield, or by Caterina Valente. 'Unchained Melody' was a favourite, as was Oscar Levant's piano music from *The Story of the Three Loves*. There were inspirational songs, like 'You'll Never Walk Alone', by Roy Orbison.

There was a genre of song that was funny and catchy, like 'Stranded in the Jungle', or David Seville's the 'Witch Doctor' ('oo ee oo ah ah, ting tang walla walla bing bang'), or Sheb Wooly's the 'Purple People Eater', or 'Itsy Bitsy Teeny Weeny Yellow Polka Dot Bikini'. There were songs with Latin American rhythms, such as the 'Blue Tango' or 'Cherry Pink and Apple Blossom White', as well as various cha-chas, rumbas and sambas, which the more progressive parents like the Carsons would dance to, and which we learned to do ourselves in dance classes at school. There were songs specifically for teenagers like Marty Robbins' 'A White Sportcoat' ('and a pink carnation') and 'A Rose and a Baby Ruth', by George Hamilton IV. There were other songs which were more mysterious, like 'Hernando's Hideaway', or 'Green Door', or 'House of Blue Lights', describing an exclusive nightlife, someplace where hot pianos were played behind closed doors, where people laughed and drank and had fun, and the only way to get in was to say 'Joe sent me.' The ambience they described, so desirable, cosmopolitan and exclusive, held tremendous attraction for us, but we couldn't experience it or find out what it was because in Winnipeg it really didn't exist.

But there we all were, for some reason we couldn't grasp, down at the Club every Friday night, milling around, going into clinches, mysteriously, gropingly, impelled towards something. Towards what? The songs we danced to only gave hints, and because they did, they were labelled 'suggestive' and condemned by parents. Songs like 'Honky Tonk', which had a heavy beat, were considered by parents to be primitive and low, as they were still associated with Negro tribal rhythms, which, by Victorian bourgeois moral standards, were inferior and animalistic.

There were lots of songs, but not one of them explained anything. The most explicit they got was to promise some kind of dream, a sparkly pink cloud that hovered ever out of reach. But the ethic of love implicit in the songs said that sex and love were supposed to go together. Sex without love was bad. Love came first, and love involved emotions, being sincere and honest and belonging to someone. But you could only dream about sex until the union was consummated by the insertion of the girl's finger into that band of gold.

A good example of the lengths to which the lyrics went to avoid being explicit, and the subsequent ambiguity, was 'Stranger in Paradise'. It is sung from the point of view of an innocent youth confronted by a woman. The assumption is that she knows more about it than he does. He asks her to take his hand, for he's a stranger in this paradise, standing starry-eyed on the threshold of a great discovery. He saw her face, and he ascended out of the commonplace into the rare, and he hangs there, suspended, now that he knows there's a chance that she cares. He pleads with her to open her angel's arms to him and not to leave him hungering alone in the dark, holding all her promise just out of reach, but to let him in so he'll be a stranger to love no more. An indication of the success of this song is that mothers liked it. Any suggestion of sexuality missed them completely.

'In the Still of the Night' (by the Five Satins) says that he held her tight in the still of the night. They could either merely have embraced in the bushes, or slept together, but you couldn't tell for sure. 'Little Darlin' (The Diamonds) says he was a wrong-a to stop-a loving her. (Are You Sincere' ('when you say you love me?'—Andy Williams) asks her if she means it. In 'Only You' (The Platters), he says she's the only one who can 'thrill' him the way she does, and she's his 'dream' come true. In 'No Not Much' (The Four Lads), he puts down his desire to have his arms around her, and says she sends him into a cool and crazy spell. In 'Teach Me Tonight', a more suggestive song, they're standing outside looking at the stars, and he says that if one should fall he'd use it to write 'I love you' a thousand times across the sky, which is a blackboard high above them. It's almost graduation, and he wants her to teach him tonight, so he can graduate. Teach him what? In 'Special Angel', he says she's sent from heaven above. In 'You Send Me', he just says she sends him. And in the Everly Brothers' 'Dream Dream Dream', he says he dreams of kissing her, but the only trouble is that he's dreaming his life away and not getting any action.

Other songs indicated that these sentiments led ultimately to the altar. In Don Cherry's 'Band of Gold', he just wants her to wear his wedding ring to prove she's his. In 'Cross Over the Bridge', Georgia Gibbs urges the young man to stop playing around and commit himself.

But dreams, spells, being sent, thrills, angels, eternity, romance, paradise—what did they all mean?

Love had to go with sex. Sex was forbidden until marriage. People could be in love, but they couldn't make it. Thus the love blew up into a romantic dream way out of proportion to reality, a dream frustrated by the taboo against premarital sex. Even if the relationship was strong and real, and not simply a romantic delusion, love was forbidden, but love was so sweet. Understandably, boys were apt to mistake the dreams, thrills and fantasies of frustrated sex for real love. It was very dangerous, sex, so most people didn't do anything. And the boy, unable to get any satisfaction, became a helpless fool over her (in the ballad 'Earth Angel' he was just a fool in love with her). In the 'Great Pretender' he was just laughing away like a clown pretending she was still around. The most a guy could do was cop the occasional feel, which triumph he would hasten back to report to the boys. The songs sung by male vocalists expressed accurately what many of the guys felt. And the spunky girl, represented by Patti Page or Teresa Brewer, would reply that if he wanted to stop his mooning around, he could marry her.

Love, the rosy dream, was good; sex was bad. Somehow, the two went together. Since we had no experience of either, we only knew there was something pink up there that we wanted, and something black down there that went with it, and you thought about one while you were doing the other. Getting emotionally involved did not mean proceeding sexually. Because sex was dirty, it lagged behind, was frustrated and furtive.

Burdened with the guilt of having to initiate this dirty thing called sex, and having it on their minds all the time, the boys, in their role of sexual predator, dressed like crooks: greasy bogie cuts, zootsuit pants and pointy black shoes; they were even called hoods, as in criminal. They looked evil, because sex was evil, and evil was sexy. Girls, on the other hand, were the fantasy objects; dressed up in straplesses and semi-formals, in piles of net, they looked like the fantasized fairy or angel, *cum* bride—pure, innocent, virtuous, unattainable. The ban on premarital sex gave girls a lot of power. If they rebuffed a kiss, they were in the right, and the boy was bad for making advances. Girls who knew that saying no was good said it a lot and learned nothing about sex.

When a girl danced with a boy, who walked her along the floor, rocking her from side to side with his eyes closed, fantasizing like crazy, she found his moist embrace repulsive and got worried. She didn't indulge any hope that there was more to boy-girl relations than getting a wet right ear from having it glued against his for three songs. As she was scraped backwards over the tiles, she might have occasion to wonder why he was so sweaty, and why he was trembling and clutching her so tightly. And if he was so bold as to press his body close to hers, her brow might furrow as she wondered about the hard pole he was carrying inside his pants, which, of course, she dexterously and modestly avoided.

Nobody could explain sex to you. You had to do it. So people groped.

If two people liked each other, and were friends, they might end up going steady. People went steady more for companionship than anything else. Parents tried to dissuade kids from going steady, because they claimed they wanted the kids to meet lots of people and not just stick to one. However, underlying that line was the fear the kids would go all the way, and have their life nipped in the bud before it had a chance.

Going steady ('Young love, first love, filled with sweet emotion') was very sweet and self-conscious and painful. The couple would hold hands in public, bashfully. They danced together all night. They were always together. If he had one, the boy would give his ball jacket to the girl. She wore it over her white shirt with the collar turned up, her tunic tail hanging down behind, slopping along in her canoe shoes, the fringe of her duck-tail rubbing against the collar, cracking her gum and carrying her books in front of her. He would get himself a parka. The leather arms on the jacket were so long—it was just like having his arms around her—that the girl kept her hands warm by clenching her hands inside the sleeves, thus adding to the sloppy effect. If he had a school ring, he might give it to her. It was usually too large, which was thrilling, because it indicated that he was bigger than she was, a real man, and to make it fit her tiny finger she had to wind adhesive tape through it to make it smaller. The adhesive tape got dirty, and she then could spend hours changing it. Or they might exchange identification bracelets, he giving her a boy's one with his name on it, and she giving him a girl's one with her name on it.

Usually it was not that serious. The high school community was like several families of kids. The athletes teamed up with the pretty girls from the new houses, and the more studious types teamed up with the more studious girls in the older houses, with some cross-referencing among those who had sports or books or looks in common. People in one group went steady with one another for a while, then everybody would break up at once, and make the shift over to someone else. But in some cases, things stuck together, especially among kids who hadn't planned on going further than high school. They got attached then and there, and stayed that way, fighting and making up, until the dream of domestic bliss could come true.

In grade ten, Irene Holt was president of Miss Cruikshank's all-girls' class, which meant she was on the student council. There she became very impressed with Murray Brueckner, but he didn't notice her. The grade elevens were having a roller skating party, and Irene was going out with another boy, so she went with him. Murray was working part-time, and didn't go roller skating, just went to the party afterwards. The boy Irene went with skated in the middle where all the fancy skaters were, while Irene had a whale of a time because she couldn't skate, and had all the guys holding her up. Her date was mad at her for that, so at the party, she went up and asked Murray to dance, and danced with him all night, and then went home with her date. After that, she saw him in school and could talk to him in school. He was coaching girls' track and field, so Irene signed up, although she wasn't athletic at all. Murray, however, was in love with his motorcycle.

There was a party over at Linda T.'s, and when she and Irene were in the bathroom, she asked Irene who she liked. You weren't normal unless you 'liked' somebody. So Irene swore her to secrecy, and told her she liked Murray. Linda T. kept quiet for quite a while, but then went up to Murray one day at school and said, 'Hey, guess who likes you?' And she told him. And he phoned and asked her out. (His motorcycle was broken then.) They went to a drive-in movie. Irene's mother was very upset at her going out with a stranger, who wasn't a Boy Scout. They started going out together. In grade eleven, they were in the same room, because Murray failed. He'd been too busy doing the student council president's job while the president was busy getting good marks. Seven years of going steady later, Irene asked Murray to marry her. She said if he married her, he could run her life. He said yes.

Guys who worked part-time had old cars. They outfitted them with strips of fuzzy little balls that hung around the windows, and equipped them with passion lights, black lights on each side of the windows at the back. A car provided the opportunity to go much further into the territory of sex. A couple could go on a heavy date to a drive-in, or park on the dyke in the middle of winter and steam up the windows together. But for kids who didn't work, life was tough.

Rec room parties afforded some opportunity, though. The rec room said much about the way things worked. The room was ostensibly handed over to the kids, while still belonging to the parents. A great deal of tension surrounded the use of the rec room, because what kids wanted to use it for was not exactly recreation. There was the constant threat of the parents bursting in on their daughter being made passionate love to by some young man, and the impeccable moral standards upstairs were put in constant jeopardy by the not so impeccable behaviour downstairs. Still, the parents held their heads high, pretending they didn't know what was going on, and the rec room became a guilt-ridden refuge for kids who furtively groped their way towards sexual awareness, also pretending to the parents that nothing was going on.

Rec room parties were given under the auspices of the parents, who provided potato chips and dip, sandwiches and soft drinks and greeted the kids as they came in the door, just as they'd always greeted the little friends their daughter had over to play. The little friends would put their coats upstairs and say hello to the parents whom they were still a bit afraid of, and go downstairs, changing into little wolves as they did so.

All the lights were on when the party started off. It was awkward, but people started dancing, and slowly things would settle in. The boy would walk the girl back to her seat after a song, and if it was going well, sit down beside her. Then suddenly he slid his arm along the back of the couch, looking in the other direction. The girl would notice but, since it wasn't doing any harm, let him keep his arm there. Then his arm flopped off the back of the couch onto the girl's shoulder. She checked out that advance, but saw no harm in it, so let him leave it there.

Meanwhile, some joker flicked the lights on and off a couple of times, amid hoots of laughter. The lights flickered and finally stayed off. On the record player were The Platters, doing 'Planting Rice', or 'Yesterday', or 'Till the End of the Night', and the wallflower in charge of the records played one song over and over again. Things started to get steamy. The guys took off their jackets and danced in their shirts. His arms intertwined with the girl of his choice, a boy would move imperceptibly in the tiny dance area, sometimes pausing for a kiss and sometimes an open-mouthed one.

Meanwhile, back on the couch, the guy might have felt he wouldn't lose any ground by taking his jacket off, and quickly slapping his arm back around the girl's shoulders, he took the opportunity provided by the interruption to pull her in close to him. The calculated advances put the girl in a difficult position. If it was all right for her to snuggle close to him, was it all right for her to kiss him? How many kisses? If it was all right for him to kiss her with his mouth closed, was it all right for him to kiss her with his mouth open? If it was all right for him to French kiss her, could he put his hand on her sweater? If it was okay for him to put his hand on the outside of her sweater, what was wrong with him putting it inside her sweater? She had to make a decision with each step about how far she was willing to let him go. She didn't want to hurt his feelings. The guys were out for all they could get. These little wrestling matches went on between couples all around the room. The guy, never content to stop and rest on a plateau, always forged ahead, until the girl whispered:

'Don't, Tom.'
'Why not?'
'Because . . .'

'Because why?'
'Well, because . . .'
'Aw, come on . . .'
'Welll . . . okay.'

Or she'd find an excuse to go to the washroom, and come back and sit on the other side of the room, leaving him sitting there empty-armed, watching enviously as guys all around him seemed to score.

Necking was the more common form of sex. Necking was just kissing. Petting, however, could 'lead to something'. Petting started where necking left off—below the neck. The hand up under the sweater, inching up to rest atop the Gothic Petalburst for a moment, a finger sliding inside the 34A cup, the hand sliding around to the back to flick the fastener open, and sliding back to rest triumphantly on the bare breast. The girl would thrill to the boy's touch, and get goose pimples; she might never have been touched there before. Brassiere fasteners were the major hurdle on the course. Usually it took two hands, and he had to pretty bold to be seen at a party with both his hands up under the girl's sweater, struggling to undo her brassiere. The girl helped by holding her sweater down.

From there, the boy took her hand and put it on his fly, while he tried to slide his hand down inside her skirt, or to slip it up the skirt. Then he might unzip, and ask her to 'hold him'. There they would stop. When the lights went up, you could tell who had been doing what with whom by whose Shocking Pink lipstick he had smeared all over his mouth, and by how fast people rearranged their clothing.

Yes, that was sex. Necking parties were called 'orgies' because of the heaving breathing and the entanglement of bodies, but were orgies in name only.

Graduation

To kids in grade ten, the grade elevens appeared far more experienced than they possibly could have been with only a year's difference. We looked down at those coming up after us, and stood in awe of the sophistication of those ahead of us, but as we looked up, we also saw the poignancy of their extra year. Time was pushing them out into the world, and that added year of exposure had already partially obscured their shining youth and promise.

And so, we moved into their spot. We were the ones facing entry into the outside world. We were the ones suddenly thrust into the limelight, to fill all the roles—student council president, star athlete, most popular girl. Now we had the responsibilities of the graduating class. Competition to be in things was even fiercer than it had been the year before. There were reputations at stake. John Hodges, boy wonder, was elected student council president. Nature's absolutes began to separate friends. Smart guys who had been dallying with pretty girls realized looks weren't everything. But who you were friends with suddenly didn't matter as much as stark ability. Amid all the competition—for boyfriends, girlfriends, marks, prestige, for recognition in sports, we suddenly found ourselves feeling very much alone. It was every man for himself. You strove to be with the person you really wanted to be with, because there wasn't much time. The end of the year, as the song said, would find us gone our separate ways.

The athletes and the pretty girls began to think about getting jobs. They could hardly wait to buy a car and have their own money. And they began to look seriously at whom they were dating, as he or she might be the person to share their lives and conceive their children. Getting a job or going to university were the choices, and which to choose depended on marks. We pretty well knew how we stood in the world by how we did in school. There was only so far you could go with a fifty per cent average, and those who had one began to make preparations to cope with reality. But those with averages in the eighties hadn't yet decided what they wanted to be, as that choice would come in university.

High school lost much of its appeal the second time around. The rituals, so new and exciting the year before, became familiar and boring. Whereas the 1955 yearbook was full of enthusiasm and charm, the 1956 yearbook was a dull rerun. The 1956 *Victory's* theme was the army—the principal was the Commander in Chief, the vice-principal Adjutant General, the staff, Intelligence Officers—a theme that looks like a sideswipe at school regimentation, which as kids were becoming more independent, was grating more each day.

Formerly cliques had formed on the basis of who lived closest to whom, and who had been in the same room together; now they were shaken up, and re-formed on the basis of shared qualities and interests. Some people who had felt secure in friendships found their friends attracted to boys who shared a common interest. It was a time of being juggled around and feeling insecure and alone. We wore the same clothes to feel we belonged to someone or something, because the fear was beginning to grow that we really didn't belong anywhere, and might never again.

Grade eleven graduation ceremonies were held in Crescent Fort Rouge United Church; that the church was out of the district meant that this was really the big time. Parents, sisters and brothers were assembled in the pews and a chorus of students was ensconced in the choir loft. A procession of girls in pastel dresses they'd made or bought for the service, with corsages pinned to the shoulder, walked up the aisle single file to Grieg's 'Triumphal March' played on the organ. The girls were followed by the boys in their sports jackets and new Ivy League stovepipe pants. Mr. Scurfield delivered his remarks, and the boys' ensemble sang Handel's 'Where'Ere You Walk'. Henry Folson, a top scholar, gave the valedictory address. The girls' choir sang Mueller's 'God Who Touchest Earth With Beauty'; the guest speaker, Major General N.E. Rodger gave an address; and the mixed choir sang 'The Lord is my Shepherd'. Then came the presentation of the awards.

John Hodges, wearing a navy blue blazer and white slacks, his Bogie cut cropped short in a crewcut, received the chartered accountant's award. Cliff Leach was the winner of the sports award. To Henry Folson went the Churchill scholarship. Janice Muirhead won the girls' sports award. John Hodges won the governor general's medal, given to the top student in the graduating class of each school; but when he got the citizenship award too, a mighty cheer rose up from the audience in the pews, and he was given a standing ovation. He was truly the man of the hour.

After the ceremonies and talking to the parents, we went home to get ready for the dance. Girls had had their hair done and had semi-formals to wear. Grad was the only night of the year that we girls could stay up all night. In fact, we were supposed to stay up. We went to the graduation dance with our dates in cars decorated with streamers and carnations made out of Kleenex. We had corsages given us by the boys. We went to a dance at the school, which was thrilling, then we went on to Jack's Place or Rancho Don Carlos or home to change out of our beautiful semi-formals into jeans and went to a rec room party. At three a.m. we were getting tired, and it was getting light. We got back in the car and made the obligatory dawn pilgramage out to Lockport, a point of interest by the locks on the Red River, consisting of an amusement park and several long old wooden hot dog stands, notably the Half Moon and Skinners. It was more of an endurance test than anything. And making grad day successful had been such a big responsibility. We certainly didn't graduate sexually though. There wasn't the slightest thought of that.

IV Twenty Years Later

Twenty Years Later

After high school, which had kept everyone together, people began to drift away from one another. The guys who didn't go on to university began to get jobs, and link up with girls. Because few boys in high school had cars, the girls they married were often from Riverview and Lord Roberts schools, and sometimes had been their steadies for several years. If they got cars before they met someone, they were able to go out with girls from other districts. Apparently quite a number of the guys knocked up their girls before marrying them, but still they did marry them. Marriage was the only way to get sex, and for people who didn't go on to university, sex was pretty important. Now people saw each other at house parties. There was a lot of friction when single guys brought different girls and there were married couples there; it made the wives feel insecure about their husbands. It got boring going to these parties, seeing the same people.

Once people got working, some began to make more money than others, and that was a major factor in splitting up friendships. People who could go out and blow a hundred bucks for dinner began to go out with other people who could do the same. High school graduates went into business for themselves, or went to work for large companies which transferred them out of town. Or they married people from other cities, or people they met at work, and went in other directions. The graduates who went directly to work succumbed to the gravitational pull of home and family much earlier than those who went to university. Many settled right in Riverview, or in middle-class areas with similar cozy white stucco houses. To be married, with a home and a family, was the next thing in life to do

The girls, those from the new postwar houses in Winnipeg, are now almost without exception full-time moms at home raising their children, just as their own mothers were. In fact, high school graduates have reproduced their parents' way of life almost perfectly. They curl, play bridge, raise their kids and build their home together. They use their parents' terms, like 'home' for house, 'chap' for fellow at the office, 'gal' for girlfriend, and 'my first' for their first child. The man earns money, and the woman stays home and raises the children. Family life gives them happiness and satisfaction, and there is no barrier between them and their parents; in fact, assuming the roles of married couples gives their lives dignity and respectability and strengthens their identities. They are upwardly mobile and, because they have been working for so long, they are often now very prosperous, with snowmobiles, cottages, houses, new clothes, appliances and big cars. Their lives are lived at a basic level. They are conservative politically, disinterested in issues such as pollution or the energy crisis, and completely bypassed by the upheavals of the sixties. They just went on being their parents, because that's what they were supposed to do, and everybody else was doing it. And in most cases the responsibilities of home and family, and especially of children, have made people happy.

Some guys went on to university. But the thing about university was that there were no teachers to line you up as there had been at school. The guys took advantage of the freedom to goof off and spent their time drinking beer in the frat house instead of studying. Goofing off persuaded them that they couldn't realize their real ambition, and after flunking out once or twice, guys, having had their wits scared out of them by the spectre of low income, went in desperation into chartered accountancy, which gave them the goods to play their husband-provider role in life. Lionel Moore had an unformed desire to be a doctor. But although he got ninety-nine in human anatomy in first-year science, he flunked out, and went into chartered accountancy. He hated it, floundered around for a while and then went into radio, like his father.

It was the kids with an average of sixty per cent or over who went on to university. Because of Winnipeg's geographic isolation, it was expensive to go away to university, so most went out to the University of Manitoba, while living at home, still dependent on their parents, prolonging their adolescence, staying sexually deprived, delaying real life for the sake of higher education. At university, they were able to meet people from all across the city, but continued, some of them, to stick with their high school steady. At university, where interests and abilities determined what faculty people entered, high school pals were split up and new friendships begun. Of the people who went on to university from Churchill, quite a number are chartered accountants, one is a social worker, one a teacher, some are engineers, some are commerce graduates, one is an architect and one a writer.

People have gone to the States without hesitation. Roots didn't enter into the decision to go there. What mattered was money and opportunity, and as people had grown up in a time when the States offered the good things and when American society was a lot healthier than it is now, it looked like a positive choice. However, Sue (Struthers) and Alan Ackland, she a publisher's editor, he a Bank of America executive, who have been in the States for a number of years, still feel like Canadians and are coming back to Canada. Few people have had any compunction about working for an American branch-plant company. Canadian nationalism didn't exist when people were making the choices that determined their lives. And where there was a chance for more money, which can improve one's private life, other considerations didn't enter the picture.

The only two people from Churchill's 1957 graduation class who did postgraduate academic work are Brenda Marshall and John Hodges. It's not till I re-encountered them that I met any of the old people whose lives had been influenced by the upheavals of the sixties—the openness to various lifestyles, the political activism, the experimentation with drugs, health food and communal living.

Now that the dust has cleared away, most people turn out to be very like their parents. Most people are married. In some Winnipeg circles marriage is still the holy institution it was for their parents. Divorce is still a bad word, a condition something like leprosy. John Kemp told me that after he was divorced his friends ostracized him. When husbands came home drunk, they said they'd been out with John Kemp, and he became everyone's alibi. Wives who had come on to him when he was married turned their backs on him. He couldn't bring a strange girl to play bridge. The people who are divorced didn't appear to be particularly happy, especially those with children. But Carol Lawrence, who is divorced with no children and who now lives in Toronto, was very happy when I last met her. Children bring great happiness into people's lives, and people with children, who are married and have homes, appear the happiest. A good number of people have assembled all the pieces—a happy marriage, good income, property, children, a satisfactory career. But even if they have, there's likely a part of them that wishes for something else.

Disaster seems to have struck at random, and, contrary to what old wives say, the burdens don't seem to have fallen on the stronger shoulders. Two people of the class of '57 have already died, Doug Young of cirrhosis of the liver, and Gary Doiron of cancer. Marriage, home and family are no protection against tragedy; rather, they provide tragedies of a permanent nature. Three children in one family drowned in a backyard swimming-pool, two couples have retarded children and two children in one family died of the same fatal disease. Some of the women have had absolutely terrible times, anxious pregnancies, looking after sick babies, nervous breakdowns and then more children, after which it happened all over again.

Perhaps the reason that the sixties passed people by is that they were already living down-to-earth and identifying with their parents, had become like their parents. They hadn't explored any alternative to the kind of life they were leading at the time and they didn't relate to the experimentation that was going on. The sixties belonged to younger people who were still free. But most of the changes of the sixties were superficial ones of style, and did little more than the fifties to change the fundamental realities and patterns of family life, or social, political and economic life.

Through the Years with the Grads

A random sample of Churchill students and the directions they have taken since 1957.

Jeremy Watson is a librarian in Winnipeg; he is married and writes in his spare time.

John Kemp runs his own insurance business, Kemp Insurance, in Winnipeg. He and his wife, whom he met when Alan Ackland lined them up on a blind date in 1961, were divorced in 1971. They had two children. He lives in the family house in Wildwood Park and plays bagpipes in the Winnipeg Pipe Band.

Cliff Leach married a girl from outside the district and is a radiologist in St. Paul, Minnesota. He and his wife have two boys and live in White Bear Estates in the country.

Alan Ackland married Sue Struthers and is a vice-president of the Bank of America in San Francisco; he teaches accounts and finance at his alma mater, Foothill Junior College, where he took his master's degree in commerce. Sue works at an educational publisher's. They own a condominium and a horse named Topper (like Hopalong Cassidy's horse), have no children and are moving to Vancouver.

Henry Folson graduated in engineering from the University of Manitoba and did postgraduate work at Imperial College in London, England. He is an engineer in California.

Wayne Kochuk is a chartered accountant in Calgary.

Stan Corda works for a company in Winnipeg which sells furs in the winter and swimming pools in the summer. He is married and lives in Charleswood.

John Hodges graduated from the School of Architecture at the University of Manitoba, and later studied in London, taking a course in regional planning and urban design. He married Marianne Patchell, like himself a top scholar from Riverview and a year younger than he. They live in Calgary, where John is a partner in an architectural firm.

Jim Kerslake married Shirley Graham, also from Lord Roberts, and he is a chartered accountant in Winnipeg.

Ross Purchase is with the Great West Life, as was his father, and is married and living in St. Vital in Winnipeg.

Claude Ibbott took a science degree at the University of Manitoba, and specialized in peridontistry at Tufts University in Boston. He intended to stay in Boston, lecture at the university and practise there, but Claude is now in Regina, as Saskatchewan's only registered peridontist. He is married with one child.

Lionel Moore took grade twelve at Churchill and flunked out of first year at United College. He went into chartered accountancy and married a girl who wasn't from his own neighbourhood. Later he left chartered accountancy for radio work. He is now a staff announcer at CBC Winnipeg. The Moores have three children and own a house in St. Boniface.

Lottie Schubert took a degree in social work at United College. She married a West Indian whom she met at the College, and is now a social guidance counsellor for ten schools in Ottawa. She has three daughters.

Barbara Kaye took a B.A. at the University of Manitoba, then a year of teacher's training; she now teaches in Vancouver, is single and owns a condominium apartment.

Frances Carson graduated from the faculty of Fine Arts at the University of Manitoba, and worked in New York in display and illustration. She met a Cambridge graduate in epistemology in New York, and they were married. They moved to London and bought a house. They are now in Australia where he is working on a dictionary and Fran is a successful painter. They have no children.

Keith Davey took a B.Comm. at the University of Manitoba and is now with IBM in Montreal.

Lex Grapentine is a doctor in Ann Arbor, Michigan.

John Malo took a B.A. at the University of Manitoba. He went to Europe, came back and worked as a cook on boats going up and down the B.C. coast. Because of his fluency in languages, he became a naval radio operator. He now is managing a hotel restaurant in Vancouver.

Bob Siemens is executive secretary to the Manitoba Hospital Commission, married and living in Charleswood in Winnipeg.

Donalee Dalenger married Mike Piercy, also from Riverview, and they live with their two children in Edmonton.

Brian Trump is a teacher, married, with children, and living in Winnipeg.

Bob Jagger is a chartered accountant, married and living on Clare Avenue in Riverview.

Phil Wake is an engineer with Canadian Pittsburgh Industries in Toronto.

Phil Harris joined the RCMP, but left when all they offered him was highway patrol. He is now with B.C. Telephone, is married, has two daughters and lives in Nanaimo.

Bruce Wood married his high school sweetheart, Jackie Legge, and is a partner with Ed Young, also of the same year, in Checkerboard Realty in Winnipeg. The Woods live in St. James and have children.

Bill Watson is divorced and living in Texas.

Isobel Leslie took a degree in astronomy at the University of Manitoba. She married an engineer, and they lived in Vancouver, then in Johannesburg. She is now living in Paris.

Lenore Doern is divorced and living in Winnipeg.

Brenda Marshall took an honours' degree in English at the University of Manitoba. She attended Union Theological Seminary in New York and married Oliver Reimer, a theological student, whom she met while working in the Christian education office in Winnipeg in 1964. They are partners with two other couples in a permanent family communal farm on 100 acres of land in the Blue Mountain Resort area near Collingwood, Ontario.

Corinne Man married her high school sweetheart, Neil Peckover, and they live in Riverview.

Gail Connell is married and teaches school in Winnipeg.

Marilyn Forrest is a registered nurse in Winnipeg.

Marge Watson is the widow of Doug Young, from Lord Roberts School, who died in the late sixties.

Janice Muirhead graduated in home economics at the University of Manitoba. She married Ed Vidruk, and they went to Madison, Wisconsin, while he did his doctorate in phys. ed. They lived in a trailer, Janice sewed and taught piano, and had a baby boy, Stephen. Ed got his Ph.D. and found a job in San Francisco; in 1974, he and his wife spent Christmas with the Acklands.

Frank Misurka is a pilot with Air Canada in Toronto.

Judy Watkins is married and living in Kapuskasing, where her husband is in business with his brother.

Helen Holmes married a professional golfer and they live in Regina.

Terry Sim is divorced and living with her two children in Winnipeg. She took a degree in fine arts at the University of Manitoba, was a housewife and mother for ten years, and is now teaching art in Winnipeg.

Maureen Butterworth married Walt Pederson, her steady after high school, whom she met through her brother. He is now a chartered accountant and general manager of Merchants Consolidated, wholesalers of groceries, hardware, software and dry goods. They have three children and live in St. Vital.

Linda Thorsteinson is married and living in Toronto.

Karin Kozub is married and living in River Heights in Winnipeg. She is assistant manager of the Great West Life branch of the Bank of Montreal. She sings in the chorus of the Manitoba Opera Association, in a church choir and with the Festival Lyric Singers, a Winnipeg amateur opera group.

Irene (Holt) and *Murray Brueckner* live on Ashland opposite the Riverview Community Club. They have three children. Murray is with the data processing section of Great West Life.

Lynne Scott is married and living in Calgary.

Carol Lawrence is divorced and working for Air Canada in the computer division.

Progress

Although much in South Fort Rouge has changed, things are very much the same. Some big changes express the ideology of progress—big, blank, efficient, impersonal concrete constructions. Some local businesses which formerly were privately owned have been taken over by foreign multi-national corporations. Still, as a result of hard work, a few of the more established personal businesses and stores have survived the last twenty-five years intact. And a flurry of strange, dusty, fly-by-night efforts has sprung up between large and small. Generally the old was personal and individual, and the new is corporate and impassive. America's triumph is virtually complete.

The old pontoon bridge at the foot of Osborne Street has given way to the new St. Vital Bridge, built at a cost of $3.5 million and opened by Manitoba premier Duff Roblin in 1965. Twenty-one homes, including the Hodges' on Montague and Kozub's Kozy Korner, were razed to make way for this humming concrete span. As a result, traffic on Osborne Street is much heavier and cars can now quickly eat up the distance across the Red and out to the Trans-Canada Highway east. In spite of the convenience, long-time residents grumble about Osborne Street traffic and the sound of motorcycles roaring across the bridge in the still of the night.

On the former streetcar barn site is a new high-rise senior citizen's complex called Fred Tipping Place, after Fred T. Tipping, a teacher, and later vice-principal, of Lord Roberts School for forty years, and a long-time Winnipeg labour and political activist. Next to Fred Tipping Place, on the original site of the Fort Rouge Curling Club, stood in the winter of '74 a huge empty Loblaws store, wearing plywood blinds over its plate glass, ready to make way for a controversial new subsidized housing project. Loblaws was a victim of competitive exclusion by the cozier, more established name of Safeway across the road. And the grim grey fortress of Mr. Scurfield's day, Lord Roberts School, has been demolished and replaced by a flat dark brown brick complex, with its name in white letters mounted on the wall.

The Top is almost dead. The Beresford Apartments, which formerly housed Campbell's Drugstore, Greeves, the Osborne branch of the Winnipeg Public Library, the Aldridge and Lamb Meat Market and Austria Furs, have been purchased by Esso, which wishes to expand its gas station on the next corner. The stores are now rented without leases, and, except for Mr. and Mrs. Reiss's Austria Furs, which celebrated its twentieth anniversary in 1973, they are peculiar, temporary-looking enterprises. By the winter of 73–74, Campbell's had become the Venus Variety Shoppe, with the name in gold and black mylar letters on the window, offering assorted grotesque ceramic objects. By summer Venus had given way to Liberation Books, a radical bookstore with a scant supply of feminist, socialist and third-world literature guarded by a gentle long-haired idealist in a bush jacket. Greeves itself is now the home of Betty Lee Newton Ceramic Enterprises, called the Ceramic Greenhouse, with two or three pots in its dusty windows.

The building at the corner of Rathgar and Osborne which used to be Johnson's Pharmacy is now a used furniture store which had a fire. Next to it are two new enterprises, Ronald's Shoes and Speedwash Laundromat, in a new building, and beside that, in a new building that at first housed the new Johnson's Drugstore, then Brickman's Pharmacy, is the Fort Rouge Pharmacy where Laurie Johnson has ultimately established himself as pharmacist to South Fort Rouge. This drugstore, associated with Western Drug Marts, has successfully combined corporate and personal elements.

Riverview United Church still stands behind the lane at Oakwood and Osborne; its new Christian Education building, Marshall Hall, was dedicated in 1960 to Reverend George Marshall, Brenda's father, who died in 1957 of lung cancer. Unlike some churches in Winnipeg which are having financial problems, almost to the point of closing, Riverview's congregation is still healthy because of the neighbourhood of families it serves.

At the corner of Oakwood and Osborne, Provincial Electric is still run by Oscar the fix-it man, although the store is up for sale. Oscar still wears the same sort of khaki baseball cap with the peak turned up, round steel-rimmed glasses and parka. Mr. Esselmont's jewellery and watch repair store is still there, exactly as it was twenty-five years ago, and Mr. Esselmont still lives on

Balfour Avenue. Beside his store is Nu Ideas Unlimited, a strange
enterprise with air fresheners and little glass jars containing aro-
matic plastic flowers displayed in the window. Riverview Hardware still bears the same name and the same sign, though it has
passed from the ownership of Mr. Wright, on Ashland, to that of
Ernie Turnbull, who used to live on Balfour and is now deceased,
into new hands.

Beside it, the Park Theatre still flourishes. Since it was sold
by Mr. Besler in 1965 to the British Odeon-Morton chain, and its
identity changed to that of a quality cinema, it draws customers
from all across the city. In the winter of 73–74, it showed
Kamouraska, Truffaut's *Day for Night, Instinct for Survival,
Triple Echo* and Mel Brooks' *Blazing Saddles*, which ran from
April till August. The Park still shows monster movies on Saturday afternoons, and even in winter these draw the same lineups of
toqued, chattering kids, their breath steaming in the air. There
are lineups for the adult movies at night now too, as in other cities,
and admissions are the standard $2.50. The Beslers still live
around the corner on Baltimore Road. But Mr. Nelson, your friendly Odeon Morton manager, takes tickets, and inside there's a
concession selling the usual overpriced popcorn and chocolate
bars. The Park's original thirties decor, the work of unemployed
Depression hands, has gone; the theatre's walls have all been
painted quality black and the seats upholstered in red, and in
place of the old green curtain a sophisticated lightweight red one
swishes across the wide screen. From the thirties only the stylized
torches on the wall remain. Still, in spite of the transformation,
you know you're in the Park. There's something familiar about the
space, the smell, the way the sound moves around the room, the
way the floor slants.

The shelves of the Osborne branch of the Winnipeg Public
Library in the old Safeway location next door have been vastly ex-
panded by Canadian books. Next to the library, in the green stucco building on the corner of Baltimore Road, Keith Routley still
carries on the dental practice he's had for many years.

Ellett's is still on the opposite corner of Baltimore Road.
Not the Ellett's of yore, mind you. The candy-striped soda-
fountain image has been usurped by the Dairy Queen, the A & W
and MacDonald's. After two renovations, one in 1958 when Jack
Ellett first got a liquor licence and kicked the kids out, and
another in 1960, Ellett's has gone all coach-housey; its front window is divided up into panes, with coach lamps on either side and
a display of Diners' Club cards; inside it has red carpeting and
dark wood tables and chairs. It is now a dark little dining room of-

fering good but not expensive food, its decor based on an Early Manitoba theme, with muskets on the walls and halves of wagon wheels mounted on the dividers between seating areas. In the back dining room is a small paddle wheel, turned by real water. On the back wall of the lounge area wire Indians on horseback and buffalo cavort with coloured plywood shapes, and over the sound system comes a Lawrence Welk arrangement of 'Little Green Apples', alternating with 'Those Were the Days my Friends'.

The Top has always had a plethora of hairdressers competing for the neighbourhood curls, and now there are even more of them. Sophie's Hair Styling, the green bungalow with the pink fieldstone front where we got our pixie cuts, was closed in 1974 because of Sophie's illness, but is now back in business.

The building which housed Kozub's Park Inn and Mr. Tactfor's Tailoring is now Emilio's Grocery, an Italian store full of Romano cheese and cans of Unico products, avoided by long-time residents who fear an influx of Italians into the neighbourhood.

The Park Alleys' eight lanes seem much smaller. The same acrid smell of sweat and smoke lingers in the air, but the clientele appears older, more hardened, and the sound of balls clinking against pins mingles with the cranking of automatic pinsetting machines. Mr. Bradshaw has sold out and retired to Texas.

The Thunderbird Mixed Billiard Lounge next to the alleys is the new focus for kids at the Top. Rock music blares, while long-haired boys in T-shirts and sheepskin jackets, with cigarettes drooping from their lips, test their prowess, with nary a girl in sight. Central Geophysics next door is new, while Artistic Upholstery, established for years, still displays its chesterfield in the window.

There are hippy batiks in the windows of the Overlook Apts. The former Jewel Store at Jubilee and Osborne, now called The Fresh Air Experience, specializes in backpacks, bicycles and freeze-dried foods. In the summer it does a thriving business renting canoes, and in the winter it does an even bigger business renting and selling cross-country skis.

As the rest of the world has congested, Riverview has correspondingly improved. Cut off even more by the increased flow of traffic along Osborne Street, and by the enclosing Red, Riverview remains a quiet backwater of respectable homes. House prices have gone up, and with its large lots and boulevards and its scarcity of people, Riverview has become a desirable place to live. Many long-time residents live on in their houses, preserving the valued stability of the area, and houses rarely come up for sale.

The area looks more cultivated and resolved. The original prairie seediness has been smoothed out, the boulevards sodded long ago, the crossroads paved and neatly curbed. Over twenty-five years, the trees have grown much taller, giving the area a luxurious, park-like feeling, especially on summer days when the quiet streets are dappled with sun and shade. In winter, except for the sparrows in the scrub oaks, the streets are silent and deep with snow under the brilliant blue sky; not a person walks the streets at night. In summer the well-kept lawns and gardens full of marigolds, petunias, sweet alyssum, salvias, zinnias and canna lilies brighten house walls, giving a cumulative impression of neat middle-class optimism. The 'new' houses on Wavell, Montgomery, Montague and McNaughton now look settled and cozy.

With the advent of diesel locomotives, it was inevitable that the Fort Rouge Yards would disappear. Lightning struck the car shops in 1956, setting off a spectacular fire, and the car shop personnel was transferred to Transcona. The shops closed in 1959, and, with the construction of the Symington Yards, remaining work slowed down, until in 1963, after forty-five years, the 212-foot smokestack was levelled with dynamite, bringing to a close an era of railroading in the Fort Rouge area. Part of the yards has become the site for a new Winnipeg Transit garage, housing 650 buses. To be near their work, bus drivers and mechanics moved into the homes formerly occupied by railroaders and union families. So the Lord Roberts side remains working-class.

The Elm Park Bridge remains, but is closed to all but pedestrian traffic. The area we called the Prairie between the dyke and the river has been filled and sodded and smoothed into a grassy plain called Churchill Drive Park; the lumps and bumps have been ironed out of the toboggan hills at the foot of Osborne Street, and many of the remaining 'Monkey Trails' turned into an official gravel bicycle path that follows the Red River to the municipal hospitals. Kids ride their bicycles down the path in the summer, and gather on the park benches to smoke dope. The river itself has many more pleasure boats on it, some of which are docked at a marina near Churchill High School. A paddlewheel boat with a crummy band plies the river on hot nights, its rock music competing with the flashes of heat lightning and rising wind. In the winter, toqued figures in knickers on cross-country skis langlauf down the river of chuff snow, through the bushes on the bicycle path. The dyke is no longer gravel but velvety asphalt all the way round to the school.

Churchill High School, like the rest of Winnipeg frozen solid six months of the year, is preserved like new from the day it was built, lying sprawled along Hay Street under the merciless sun which beats against the glass bricks in summer until classrooms are eighty-eight degrees and unusable. Two additions, with a total of twenty-four classrooms, have been built on behind, but the school looks exactly the same from Hay Street. Inside, the school is mellower, but impeccable. In the vast green gymnasium, two huge stylized bulldog faces glare down from the walls; during lunch hour, rock music is blasted over the P.A. system, and long-haired boys in sweat pants and T-shirts dribble basketballs around. The lockers lining the halls are no longer painted institutional grey, but bright red, green and blue. There are even more pictures of Winston Churchill around than there used to be.

The principal's office is now guarded by three secretaries. When this office was vacated by Scuff in 1965, an annual scholarship was set up in his honour. Scuff went on to be assistant superintendent of the Seven Oaks School District, then retired to his home, his wife, his children and grandchildren and his begonias. I went to see him in the winter of 1974. At seventy-four he looked exactly the same as always, but he was wearing the cardigan and slippers of a retired gentleman, padding around in the living room of his home. He remembered the first class at Churchill well, the good students especially, whose father had died, whose mother was pushy, who was earnest and who was conscientious. When he pointed his finger at me, I knew who was principal. In October of 1974, Mr. Scurfield died of complications following surgery.

Since 1965, the principal's office at Churchill has been filled by Scuff's right-hand man, Zorro (so called because he was everywhere at once), i.e. Mr. W. J. Madder, a calm, crisp gentleman with greying temples, glasses and the same thin line of moustache he always wore. His face is orderly and conservative, though the shoulder vents in his impeccable grey suit betray a hint of the swinging liberal he might have been, if it weren't for the school system. On the brick wall behind him is the obligatory picture of Winston Churchill beside an official portrait of Queen Elizabeth with the bathing beauty blue ribbon across her front. The chair opposite Mr. Madder's desk is frightening in its power to turn anyone sitting in it into a student with that old father-fixation attitude toward authority. But unlike Scuff Mr. Madder is not an overpowering principal. Rational and kindly, he wards off the educational greyness that threatens his personality with a sympathetic twinkle in his eye.

From an original population of 861, the number of students at Churchill peaked in 1966 at 1635, with the coming to high school age of the postwar boom babies. Now, owing to the movement of families from the area out to the suburbs, and to the decline in the birth rate, the attendance has shrunk back to 1200. The population of suburban schools has grown, while Churchill's has declined, and Churchill is now considered almost an inner-city school.

Although the school looks the same, things have changed at Churchill. The old narrow-minded rigidity has opened to the outside world and its variety, and many of the changes have been in the direction of more individual freedom for the student and much more help for him. However, it's hard to know if the changes are real and basic, or if they are just superficial trimmings, the old ways jazzed up to give the appearance of progress.

Things at least have different names. Home rooms are called teaching stations. There's 'team teaching', and 'contract teaching'. Classrooms are now equipped with overhead projectors, so instead of drawing his diagram laboriously on the chalk board and getting it all smudged, the teacher can draw it permanently on an acetate sheet, and project it on a screen behind him. There are filing cabinets full of research material, extra reference books and closed circuit TV; some rooms are wired for sound. Other rooms have carpets and drapes, bulletin boards that can be moved around and used as dividers, and movable chairs and tables that will fit together in a variety of formations.

The effort by the school to provide a programme more suited to the individual was generated, says Mr. Madder, not by student demands, but by the teachers who saw students struggling with the material, but couldn't help them. The problem now with trying to give so much individual attention, he said, is that the demands on the teacher's time are almost impossible. But the general idea is to offer the student a variety of choices and influences so he can, you guessed it, do his own thing. The student council president and vice-president and the editor of the school newspaper are on the school's budget committee, though all policy is subject to staff ratification. The painting of the lockers in different colours was carried out on student initiative. Students seem to be considered a little bit more trustworthy than they were twenty years ago.

The old-fashioned school tea has been superseded by a much more sophisticated event, the Novemberfest, held in November, perhaps to avoid association with Octoberfest beer. Instead of the large tea room in the gymnasium, different kinds of refreshment and entertainment are provided in several different rooms—an English tea room, a coffee house, a French sidewalk cafe, with students doing the can-can, games of skill and chance in the lunch room, a supper bar with a cold plate. The inevitable sale of home baking takes place, but instead of a white elephant sale, there is a sale of plants and terraria grown in the school. School dances are a losing proposition and aren't well attended. Rock bands cost too much, and records are unthinkable.

No longer is there one single guidance teacher advising students to join the army, as Charlie Martin used to do. Instead, there are now four full-time guidance instructors who help students with their personal problems, in a special guidance office complete with magazines, several private cubicles for individual consultations and one large room for group discussions. The Child Care Clinic sends both a social worker and a psychiatrist around to the school. 'Oh,' sighs Mr. Madder, 'we have our drug abuse problems and alcoholism.' Drugs? Would Winston Churchill have endorsed drugs?

Mr. Madder showed me the huge barren lunchroom, the automotive shops, the video-taping equipment and the music room (where Henry Folson's sister Eileen is now the teacher), overflowing with double basses, violins and cellos and set up with music stands for sixty-five musicians. We looked at the library with its 'liquid carrels' wired for tape recorders and audio-visual equipment. We ran into some of the teachers of old: John Wright, who was vice-principal, his hair white, looking healthy and well put together in his Black Watch tartan jacket, gave Mr. Madder a look of long-standing respect and affection; Mr. Bell, the physics teacher, was dapper in a checked jacket; Mr. Curry the chemistry teacher still had his white lab coat, round ruddy face, rimless glasses and shy smiling James Stewart manner, exactly the same; Mrs. Bond was exactly the same in her cardigan sweater and straight skirt. They were all exactly the same; time had done absolutely nothing to alter their essential beings. Standing in the halls, they were like those life-sized cardboard figures you sometimes see in drugstores, they could have been exact replicas of themselves. But if they were still the same, how much could the school have changed?

Room 8, Miss East's home room of 1955, was unchanged. There were the green blackboards and the wood of the 'single-piece arborite desks', slightly darker with age, a still life frozen forever in time, while the bright sunlight bounced off the snow and slanted in through the 'vision strip' as it always did. The minute hand on the clock overhead clicked on its interminable way. The only change was that the old wooden teacher's desk at the front of the room on the left, instead of bluntly facing the class head on, had mysteriously opened like a door to stand at an *angle.*

On the honours board outside Mr. Madder's office, there were our pictures—mine (with a pixie cut) for a scholarship, John Hodges's picture twice, for an award and for being school president. I scrutinized the most recent pictures; the award-winning kids looked much the same; short haired, clean-cut, pimply, awkward. As I bade good-bye to Mr. Madder, he said that one of the things about being principal was that you spent more time in administration and less time in personal contact with the students. He confessed he missed being called Zorro.

At the end of the lunch hour, kids crowded against the glass in the front foyer and overflowed into the hall. A boy hawked tickets to a performance by the hypnotist Reveen. The kids were awfully short. The girls wore jeans and T-shirts, like the boys, not a tunic or Kitten sweater among them. The boys all had long hair. They milled around instead of lining up. The old teachers stood like rocks awaiting the noisy onslaught as it poured into the halls and flowed around them. I walked home, down the sidewalk on Hay, in the brilliant sunshine, feet crunching in the cornstarch snow, remembering how worried we used to be that we'd freeze our legs beneath our short tunics before making it home. It was as cold as it ever was.